STILL STANDING

Inspiration From People with Long-Term Abstinence from Alcohol and Drugs

By Barb Chrysler

for

Rehab**Helpdesk**.org

NANSHE
PUBLISHING

Copyright © 2016 Rehab Helpdesk.org
All rights reserved, including the right to
reproduce this book or portions thereof in
any form.

Nanshe Publishing
PO Box 20111 Pioneer Park, 123 Pioneer Drive,
Kitchener, ON, Canada N2P 1L9
www.nanshepublishing.biz
www.barbchrysler.biz

ISBN: 978-1-988324-03-6
http://rehabhelpdesk.org

For every 500 books printed Nanshe Publishing will
donate trees in areas most needed.

ACKNOWLEDGEMENT

With appreciation to Howard for funding this project and gratitude to the individuals who shared their stories.

Additional acknowledgement to Subtrano Deb for the book cover design, Bhavnish Kanojjia for inside book design, and Jay Allman for editing assistance.

TABLE OF CONTENTS

Alcoholism and Hope 1

Factors Associated with Long-Term Recovery 2

    Readiness and Desire to Change 5

    Association with 12-step Groups 7

    Commitment to Abstinence 12

    Having Something to Lose 15

    Community Support and Making New Friends 15

    Working a 12-step Program 26

    Faith in God or a Power Greater than Themselves.. 33

    Sponsor, Sponsors Someone, Does Charity Work 34

    Significant Reason to Start and Maintain Sobriety. 35

    Received Treatment 38

    Intensity of 12-step Programs 40

    Sugar 42

    Exercise 44

    Dealing with Other Addictions 45

    Behavioural Change 47

    Gratitude 49

Stories of Long-Term Recovery 50

    Tom – 33 years 51

    John – 34 years 67

    Paul – 20 years 87

    Diane – 34 years 114

Mike – 39 years	139
Sue – 37 years	160
Karen – 32 Years	174
Betty – 35 years	194
The 12-steps of Alcoholics Anonymous	208
References	211
Rehab Helpdesk	220

ALCOHOLISM AND HOPE

Sobriety was the greatest gift I ever gave myself.
— Rob Lowe

After working in the mental health and addiction system for over thirty years, always with the question of how to facilitate change, I have come to believe that the Alcoholics Anonymous (AA) program is one of the most effective methods to achieve behavioural change. This book attempts to identify factors that lead to long-term abstinence. A combination of research and interviews was used to compile this volume.

The stories tell what it was like for individuals prior to entry into Alcoholics Anonymous, and what they felt contributed to their achievement of long-term sobriety. These stories are inspiring and demonstrate that it is possible to have a different life style.

I just woke up one day and decided I didn't want to feel like that anymore or ever again. So I changed.

— Anonymous

FACTORS ASSOCIATED WITH LONG-TERM RECOVERY

And when we have that moment, clarity, truth, and commitment-- the whole world, in all its crazy beauty-- opens up to us.

— Anonymous

Much of the research on addiction focuses on the nature of substance use and less on the recovery process. This book is focused on recovery and summarizing research on factors associated with long-term recovery. It also provides inspiration from interviews conducted with eight individuals with long-term sobriety, one with twenty years and seven of them with over thirty years. This book is fairly unique, as the interviews are with people who have such long-term abstinence. The interviews and research illustrate that the recovery experience changes over time, making shifting demands on individuals.

There is good news: Many people can and do recover from addictions. The summary of the research and interviews provides insight into key factors that appear to help individuals maintain long-term sobriety. Many people who beat addiction build a wonderful life. This book outlines factors associated with the recovery process. Some of the influencing factors are:

- readiness to do whatever is needed to stay sober
- joining a 12-step group
- commitment to abstinence
- having something to lose
- community and social support
- prioritizing sobriety
- working the twelve steps
- seeking advice from role models, sponsors, and professionals if one is having difficulties.

- › quitting all mind-altering substances, although some prescribed mental health medication may be required
- › eliminating or reducing sugar from the diet
- › exercise and
- › having gratitude.

Readiness and Desire to Change

Individuals who were interviewed talked about being ready to quit drinking, and that relapses were partially the result of not being willing to admit they were an alcoholic. Alcoholics Anonymous, perhaps one of the first 12-step groups, published a program of recovery and discussed the importance of readiness in the first step, which is, "we admitted we were powerless over alcohol and that our lives had become unmanageable." Since then, the importance of readiness has been theorized in what is called the *Stages of Change*. Motivation to change is viewed as a critical factor in inducing people to seek and comply with efforts to recover from addictions (DiClemente and Scott, 1997).

"My dry date is December 2, 1995. It is my second dry date. My first dry date was January 19, 1994. There was stuff going on in my brain. I was thinking, am I really an alcoholic? Then one day, just after my mom died, someone ordered some beer and he asked me, do you want one? I drank it, and as soon as it touched my lips I had that feeling and craving for alcohol.

In 1995 it all blew up, the shit hit the fan when I got home. So since December 2, 1995, I've been sober, and I went back to AA meetings. I can never safely use again. That realization is the biggest difference from the other times before. I didn't want to accept it, but when I picked up a drink I began where I left off before I became abstinent." (Paul)

Association with 12-step Groups

Of the many factors involved in long-term recovery, one that seems to be prevalent is the addict's or problem drinker's involvement in Alcoholics Anonymous. Moos and Moos (2006) explain that AA, or 12-step treatment, is associated with the theory of behavioural economics. They interviewed

461 subjects who sought help for alcohol-related problems on their own. These researchers discovered that behavioural economics theory may predict the amount of time that a person with problems surrounding alcohol use stays in remission. This study also suggests that 12-step treatment is correlated with an increased likelihood for long-term recovery.

The first AA group started in 1935 with two members, and the growth of this movement has been significant, with worldwide active membership in 2014 at 2,040,629 the movement has over 115,326 groups (AA, 2016). In research on short-term abstinence, affiliation with 12-step fellowships has been found to be helpful in maintaining sobriety (Humphreys et al., 1994 and 1999; Laudet et al., 2000; Timko et al., 1995 and 2000). Additionally, another research study on people with an average of over twelve years in recovery found that the key factors that individuals reported as significant to establish and maintain their sobriety was affiliation with 12-step organization and the adverse consequences of substance use (Laudet et al., 2000).

The interviews conducted for this book with individuals with long-term sobriety all verified the importance of a 12-step recovery program. People who were interviewed did talk about changing the frequency of meeting attendance over time, and sometimes even taking a break from meetings for a while. Those who took a break often came back to meetings, saying that the principles and fellowship of the program helped them in their day-to-day life. Often while people were not attending meetings they were working in the field or doing volunteer work or had friends and family who were also sober. Sometimes they attended less due to aging and mobility issues. However, some of those interviewed still attended three meetings a week.

"AA literally came overnight from something I knew nothing about to my guide and mentor. I couldn't get enough of it, and loved every meeting I went to." (Lionel)

"I still go to two or three meetings a week. I never took a hiatus." (Sue)

"The fellowship of AA helped me achieve this length of sobriety. Even in my first years I was surrounded with the AA fellowship. I met my wife there; she has twenty-seven years abstinent. AA people surrounded me." (Karen)

"The all-important factor for me is going to meetings. I need to go to meetings. I remember one man who had a relapse said, it's like I took the most precious thing I had and it's never come back." (Mike)

"Alcoholics Anonymous was part of the detoxification treatment, and I remembered at the first meeting having the feeling that anything was now possible for me to achieve." (Diane)

"When I walked into the meeting and felt the magic, I felt that people understood me and that they wanted me to get the program." (Sue)

"I went every morning to AA and in the evenings too." (Betty)

"At the meeting the people welcomed me even though I was hung over and drunk. There was a person who welcomed me. He had a calm voice and steady hand. I developed that calm voice and steady hand." (John)

Commitment to Abstinence

The first step toward getting somewhere is to decide you are not going to stay where you are.

— ANONYMOUS

Researchers found that commitment to total abstinence was important to obtaining short-term recovery (Hall, 1991). Interviews conducted for this book verified that people with long-term recovery had made a commitment to attain abstinence. People sometimes talked about using different methods to try to control drinking and or drug use before committing to abstinence.

"Early in my sobriety, the first ten years, if something really bad happened and I got angry I would say, fucked if they were going to get my sobriety. Now I'm thinking that when I'm going to meet my master, I'm going to do it sober." (Karen)

"I was very committed to my sobriety and would say to myself and others, come hell or high water I am not going to drink. It was a mindset that was important because drinking was not an option." (Diane)

"When I came into the program, I started planning my first talk and planning the first twenty-five years." (Mike)

"If I got the urge, I would say, I will drink tomorrow, but tomorrow never comes. Just for today helped." (Sue)

"I went to a meeting, and I made a decision, and there was no changing my mind. I don't think I've had any doubt that I'm an alcoholic." (Lionel)

"I never looked back. There is alcohol in the kitchen and it doesn't bother me. I don't need it. I think a lot of people who are in and out of the program, they want to drink, but for me, I didn't want to drink again." (Lionel)

Having Something to Lose

Scholars have found that individuals who perceive they have 'something to lose' (e.g., family, friends, employment, health, freedom) if substance use persists were inspired to change. Individuals who have this perception are more likely to have long-term abstinence (e.g., Costello, 1975 et al.; Havassy et al., 1993; Vaillant, 1995). Individuals recovering from alcohol and substance use often talk about 'hitting bottom' and frequently mention it as a pivotal point and the beginning of their efforts to change and recover. When they reach this point they have a realization of how much they have lost to their addictions, such as family, friends, jobs, home, health, and self-respect.

They usually see where their life will go if they continue this path and realize the need to make a dramatic change. This turning point often awakens people to the need to find help, and they begin to search for something to assist in their change. The negative consequences of substance use have previously been identified as a significant predictor of short-term abstinence (Laudet et al., 2002). Those interviewed for this book also talked about hitting bottom and feeling there was something to lose or that they had already lost things important to them.

"Woke up in a dirty, filthy room with prison bars. I was in a suit. I didn't know how I got there. I asked a guard, how did I get here? He said, a hit and run. From eleven at night until seven the next morning I thought I killed someone. I couldn't believe that I, a person who wanted to be a good father and husband and a community man who worked with people who were disabled, and had been written about in the paper, was in this place. If I was drunk and killed someone and left, I made a decision I would rather die. I went to a meeting and

I made a decision, and there was no changing my mind." (Lionel)

"I was thirty-five, married with three teenagers. I became unemployed and went through a fifteen-month period of unemployment. I couldn't buy a job. They blacklisted me. I had to start over.... Basically relied on fears." (Mike)

"I got into a huge fight with my wife and was having a custody issue with my daughter. In 1995 it all blew up, the shit hit the fan when I got home. She said, I'm going to call and get you arrested, I'm going to leave you and take the house or you need to call this counselor in one hour. Then I thought I'm going to lose everything. Then I thought, oh my God, that is true, everything they said in AA, and I phoned the counselor. The counselor told me, you should go back to AA or NA." (Paul)

Community Support and Making New Friends

Social-learning theory holds that behavior is learned, and it stresses the importance of role models. It suggests that people will emulate the actions they see, proposing that an essential factor to long-term recovery is to surround yourself with well-adjusted individuals who make good choices. Researchers have found that social and community support was instrumental in assisting people with an average of over twelve years in long-term recovery (Laudet et al., 2002). Other researchers found that the 12-step groups and working the twelve steps are especially important for people who had a large social network of people who supported their drinking before they quit (Fiorentine, 2000).

Another key factor that is associated with long-term recovery involves what type of people addicts have in their social network. Not only is the quality of relationships important in recovery, as discussed above with social control theory (Moos & Moos 2007), but the activities and behaviors of people within the social networks of addicts are crucial in long-term recovery as well (Polcin, Korcha, Bond & Galloway, 2010). It is often difficult for substance users to end relationships with friends who also drink.

Polcin, et al., (2010) found that addicts who have friends in their social networks with heavier drinking problems are less likely to report abstinence and tend to demonstrate increased alcohol and drug use, as well as higher scores on the DSMIV checklist.

Polcin, et al., (2010) also found that subjects who reported a higher percentage of people in their social networks who had drinking problems, or drank heavily, were less likely to have ninety days of sobriety at one year and three-year follow-up interviews. Those who reported a higher percentage of friends who encouraged them to drink less were more likely to state they had ninety days of abstaining from alcohol.

The study conducted by Humphreys, Coos and Cohen (1997) also pinpointed the importance of social relationships in long-term recovery. It was discovered that subjects who had higher quality relationships with extended family members were more likely to remain abstinent. It has also been emphasized that closer relationships with family members, friends, and co-workers tended to lead to a healthier psychosocial functioning and decreased drug and alcohol use. These two statistics are supported by social control theory (Moos & Moos 2007).

Research indicates that both AA, or 12-step involvement, and making wise choices regarding the people addicts socialize with are key factors in maintaining long-term sobriety. The quality of the relationships in the lives of individuals with alcoholism also plays a role in long-term recovery.

This finding was supported by the individuals interviewed for this book. This support comes not only from people in 12-step recovery programs but from family and friends and others who are aware of and support the change. Some of those interviewed talked about having a loving family. The support provided by these people offers encouragement, hope, and strength to get through difficult times.

Additionally, people talked about the importance of changing their environment and removing themselves from individuals who drank or places where there were alcohol or drugs. After they removed themselves from these places and people they focused on making new friends and undertaking new hobbies.

"Peers and role models are important. I have good memories of old timers. I enjoy being around people." (Mike)

"Meeting and socializing with new AA friends was very special. I have fond memories of those days and feel the friendships made were very extraordinary. There was a shared bond. When I went to the detoxification centre I removed myself from my old friends and I moved and began to build a new network at meetings." (Diane)

"The fellowship of AA helped me achieve this length of sobriety. Even in my first years I was surrounded with the AA fellowship. I met my wife there; she has twenty-seven years. AA people surrounded me. That feeling of belonging got me to stay. That is my life. There is no way to separate it." (Karen)

"I realized that I was hanging around a bad crowd, so I gave up all my friends from the past." (Mike)

"I would not have made it without the help of a lot of people." (Lionel)

"I made lots of friends, women particularly; I always thought if they are alcoholic it's okay for me to be; because they were people I respected and looked up to. We had so much fun together and became a real club. Some men we socialized with too, but mostly with women, they were so nice and I admired them so much. We had a lot of nice women in our AA group meeting." (Betty)

Working a 12-step Program

Researchers have found that ninety percent of individuals who had achieved at least twelve years of sobriety used the twelve steps as an active part of their life. Eighty percent of those in that research study still attended AA, and thirty-five percent attended Narcotics Anonymous. The frequency of meetings declined as abstinence increased. This was echoed in the interviews conducted for this book. All those interviewed for this book had found a 12-step program helpful, and while the frequency of meetings attended decreased or there were breaks from meetings, it was generally recognized as important in the recovery process.

There is widespread acceptance of AA. It has been estimated that ninety percent of people who participated in a population-based questionnaire endorsed AA as an intervention of choice for alcohol issues (Caetano, 1987).

"I went to a meeting and the thought came across to me that for once in my life I should do what people told me. So for once in my life I did what people told me. Never before did I take direction, not as a child, teen, or adult. I wanted to do it my way." (Mike)

"After detoxification I continued to go to AA meetings regularly and was very involved in AA, helping set up meetings, making sandwiches, cleaning up, service, and greeting newcomers. As a young woman, I was able to help and reach out to other young women. I strictly followed what I was advised to do: getting a sponsor, completing the steps, not making any serious decisions or changes for a year, sponsoring others, not becoming involved in a relationship for a year, and was cautious for five years about making changes. AA literature was always in my purse, and I read it religiously." (Diane)

"The steps became a part of my life. I began a home group study with a person with long-term sobriety of five years. This was what they were doing in Windsor. The big thing was the emphasis on the fourth and fifth step and we were not going to move on unless we all completed the fourth and fifth step it was like pulling teeth. The day I started writing the fourth it was like I had a magic pen I couldn't stop writing. After I finished I went with another person and we sat in the back of his car behind the ski hill and talked for two hours. I didn't feel elated or relieved. When I came to the AA program it wasn't easy. There were kid problems, domestic problems, life problems. The program has always been able to help us through." (Mike)

"I never did go through the steps until another man in AA and I joined a study session, and that was when I did the fourth step, but I never really did a step with anyone until the fifth step. I was about seven years sober." (John)

"I walked away from meetings for a while. After we bought the house we had problems in a group and we wandered away. I still had AA people coming in and out of my life. My sponsor had died. But I went back to a meeting and there was a woman there at her first meeting, and suddenly I felt at home and became active all over again." (Karen)

"Six or seven years ago I found out that during the times I wasn't going to meetings

I did a lot of damage and I wasn't aware of it. I wasn't aware of the problems I was creating in our life." (Karen)

"I frequently go through the steps. Now it usually takes the form of working the steps with a newcomer. For the first twenty years I had step study groups in my home. The last one was five or six years ago. Right now I am working with a new sponsee and we are going through the steps - step by step, and she shares and I share. Each time I do them it brings me deeper into myself and I am always learning something new about myself. Recently learning that there was something from my childhood that would push a button. It shocked me at the time because I thought I dealt with everything there was. I was able to take that little child and embrace her and give her the love she didn't feel she got when she was growing up. For me, it is important to always be working the steps. There is always something new to learn. If I didn't go to meetings I might not drink but my thinking would get off." (Sue)

"The steps are beautifully written and easy to misunderstand. Step one, two, three, you can't get anywhere until you admit you have a problem. Everyone that gets to that point has a problem." (Lionel)

"Alcoholism is a disease. It is step one: Be brave enough to admit it." (Lionel)

Faith in God or a Power Greater than Themselves

"The key to the recovery process is a spiritual experience as the result of practicing the daily discipline of the 12 steps, a process which evokes a psychic change sufficient to recover from this disease" (Sandoz, 2014). This statement published by researchers in the Department of Psychology at Troy University was validated by those who participated in the interviews for this book.

"I would not have made it without belief in God." (Lionel)

"I really went down hill. I was not taking care of the house and my boys were worried about me. Throughout this time I kept praying, and praying, and praying." (Betty)

"Learning that I had to change my concept of God, because how could I have a relationship with someone I was hiding from? Prayer and meditation every day is important and I am extremely disciplined with that and do that about ½ hour." (Sue)

Sponsor, Sponsors Someone, Does Charity Work

In one research study (Laudet et al., 2002), sixty percent of individuals with over twelve years of abstinence had a sponsor, and fifty-two percent sponsored someone. Sponsoring and having sponsors was also discussed in the interviews conducted for this book.

"Working with new people is another important component. I am sponsoring eight people now. They are sober from two years to thirty-five years. I just love them and they inspire me, and that is what I need to keep out of Sue's head." (Sue)

"My sponsor is ten years older than me, she is ninety-three and has seven years more sobriety than me." (Betty)

Significant Reason to Start and Maintain Sobriety

Research has found that individuals quit drinking for the following reasons:

> worsening consequences of alcohol and drug use
> reinforcement of peers/family/friends who support the decision
> 12-step groups

- › criminal justice issues such as alcohol and drug related accidents and arrests
- › referral from individuals working in recovery
- › desire to recover
- › having a child and wanting to be responsible parent
- › a higher power or spiritual experience.

The attached stories echo the above reasons for going to AA. Some people had multiple reasons for making the decision to move forward with their lives and maintain that commitment.

"In 1995 it all blew up, the shit hit the fan when I got home. She said, I'm going to call and get you arrested, I'm going to leave you, and take the house, or you need to call this counselor in one hour. Then I thought, I'm going to lose everything." (Paul)

"My son, the youngest, is a counselor and he has groups with AA men and learned a lot about alcoholism. When his father died, he was eleven and was looking after me. It was less than a year ago that he said, Mom, did I ever thank you for getting sober; you have no idea how much it meant to me" When we went to the cottage, there were so many things that I was able to do with him, if I had not have been sober, he would have missed so much. To come and thank me it was a tearjerker. They don't worry about me. Sobriety has an impact. I owe it to God and AA. I'm a staunch AA member." (Betty)

"What happened was I became a father once I was sober, and not long after I became a grandfather. I found as the family grew I started to like my place. I began to like being a husband, grandfather, and father." (Mike)

Received Treatment

In one research study, which utilized treatment facilities to recruit study participants, two-thirds had used other treatment programs in addition to 12-step recovery programs (Laudet et al., 2002). In the small sample used for this book several individuals went to counseling or treatment although there was one who never went to anything beyond AA.

"I went for treatment for co-dependency. Going to a family treatment program was hugely helpful and assisted me to establish better boundaries. I can't do anything for others. I can only encourage things." (Sue)

"Desperate, I went to the doctor to seek help. I was put on Antabuse and several mood-altering drugs, including Valium. The effect of the prescription drugs on my mental health was significant. At a party, someone gave me a drink, telling me it was water but it was not. Quickly, I became very ill and ended up in the hospital, in the Detoxification Centre. It was a non-medical Detoxification Unit, and all I received for the withdrawals was L-Tryptophan. The hallucinations were again part of my withdrawal." (Diane)

"They asked me about my drug and alcohol use, and I didn't tell them. Later I went to an addiction counselor in the basement of a mall, and I told him my story. I was low, my hair was long, I was out of control. They told me I should stop and I went to AA." (Paul)

Intensity of 12-step Programs

Twelve-step programs offer more intensity than treatment programs. AA meetings are generally widely available and offer morning, afternoon, and evening options depending on where you live. Both research studies and the people interviewed identify the need for individuals to attended meetings very frequently for years. Most formal treatment options are short-term counseling programs that may be available once a week, have wait lists, and may not be offered for a long duration. In-patient treatment may be provided for several weeks with only once-a-week follow-ups possibly being offered after. People choose to stay involved in 12-step recovery programs beyond the initial recovery period suggesting that the benefits are long-term.

"Attending maybe six hundred meetings a year, two meetings a day, I got re-engaged in recovery for lots of good reason." (Paul)

"Going to meetings, I am reminded of what it was like, how hard it was, and how painful it was when I came in. I still go to two or three meetings a week. I never took a hiatus." (Sue)

Sugar

Current research has illustrated that a great number of substance-dependent people have a sweet craving, particularly for foods with a high sucrose concentration. Furthermore, research has shown that in some individuals the brain's release of euphoric endorphins and dopamine is similar to drugs of abuse when sugar-rich foods or drinks are consumed. Withdrawal, craving, tolerance, and sensitization have been documented in research studies. Additionally, the studies seem to illustrate that individuals with narcotic dependence have a cross-sensitization with sugar addiction. Observations have shown larger risk to a strong sugar preference in biological children of alcoholic parents, especially alcoholic fathers, which may result in some individuals having an eating disorder. Recent research over the last two decades is suggesting that specific genes may underlie the sweet cravings in substance dependent individuals, as well as in the children who have a father who is an alcoholic. Additionally, there seems to be certain shared genetic markers between bulimia, alcohol dependence, and obesity (Fortuna, 2010).

"I need to be careful with how much coffee or sugar I use." (Paul)

"I'm still addicted to chocolate and ice cream and sugar in general. If I have a box of chocolates I say I'm going to have one, but I won't." (Sue)

"I was treated for a minor eating disorder and depression. Especially early in sobriety I would binge eat; which I found was sometimes triggered by past memories. I received six months of outpatient counseling for this. Deserts and chocolate cannot be kept in my home. Within twenty-four hours they would be gone." (Diane)

Exercise

Exercise helps control the circadian rhythm and is an extremely successful way to help decrease alcohol intake. Researchers have found that exercise supports decreased drinking (Trivedi et al.,

2011; Murphy et al., 1986; Sinyor et al., 1982; Brown et al., 2009).

"Exercise, weight lifting, aerobics, and cycling were vitally important, and I sometimes spent up to three hours a day doing these activities." (Diane)

Dealing with Other Addictions

Some of the people who were interviewed for this book, talked about being cross- addicted to drugs and alcohol. Others smoked and gave up smoking, and some discussed sugar addictions. Additionally, some talked about being addicted to members of the opposite sex.

"I've had issues with sex, and sex was just as good as a drug. The feeling of being connected to a woman - I confused it all…. I always have issues of monitoring excessiveness like golfing or eating. If one thing is good, a thousand is better. Addiction is not just about substance, it's about the brain being caressed with enjoyable feelings." (Paul)

"Early in sobriety, I had to deal with relationship issues through counseling. At times, I referred to men as being my favourite mood-altering drug. There was often a lack of wisdom in my choices. Although I went to counseling for this, it is an area I do not feel I addressed to a point of satisfaction. I am currently comfortably single and have been that way approaching three years." (Diane)

"I quit smoking, I went from one pack a day to three packs a day, and I couldn't breathe. Using the twelve steps I quit smoking. Chocolate and ice cream, I still occasionally will have it but I'm aware of my powerlessness and make sure there is not too much in the house." (Sue)

Behavioural Change

Researchers have found that behavioural change was important in maintaining abstinence. These changes included decreasing, avoidance or removal of exposure to drinking, reliance of several reinforcement techniques, and seeking information and advice about substance use and alcohol-related difficulties (Snow et al., 1994).

"In recovery I've completely changed my whole social network. I don't go to darts, the people there are there to play darts and to drink. I started playing golf and began coaching soccer and refereeing hockey. I have to work recovery in my new recreational activities. After sports events some people would drink in the car. I felt uncomfortable, so I brought my own drinks and pop and made sure I was safe. When I say to my wife, I need to go, there are no questions asked." (Paul)

"When I went to the Detoxification Centre, I removed myself from my friends and environment and began to build a new network at meetings. I was just as tired of the lifestyle as I was of alcohol. It is my belief that the desire to leave the lifestyle at the same time helped me a great deal to maintain abstinence." (Diane)

Gratitude

Gratitude for AA was a common thread in all the interviews conducted for this book.

"AA was the biggest blessing in my life." (Sue)

"I'm so grateful, and my children are thankful that I found AA. I never prayed so hard in my whole life to try and get sober; it's the hardest thing to do. Sobriety has an impact. I owe it to God and AA. I'm a staunch AA member." (Betty)

STORIES OF LONG-TERM RECOVERY

Don't judge or look at my past too hard. I don't live there anymore.

—Anonymous

Alcoholism got in the way of who I was supposed to be. Recovery made me the person I was supposed to be.

—Paul

Tom – 33 years

When I look back on my childhood, I see a nervous and fearful little kid I call 'little Tommy,' always anxious, worried about the school bullies and life in general. But in my early teens I grew to be both tall and fast and began to excel at track and field.

As a seventeen-year-old kid from a poor family growing up during the Depression in Montreal, I applied for and got accepted into Military College and all of a sudden I was an officer in training in the Royal Canadian Air Force. This enabled me to go into a program in which the government paid for a Science degree, a degree in Mechanical Engineering, and Flight Training. Five years later I was a fighter pilot and test pilot for the F86 Sabre jets with NATO in Europe.

Leaving the Air Force after eight years, I took up a position in Aerospace Engineering. The company was growing rapidly and opportunities opened. I had the motivation to work hard I was promoted often, progressing from a junior engineer to supervisor to the chief of quality control and I was still in my early thirties.

On the outside I was successful, happily married to a wonderful lady and had four great kids. But inside I was still 'little Tommy' often anxious and uptight. I wanted to be liked and be successful. I wanted to be known as a good father, a good husband and a good community member. At thirty I went back to school for a year and switched my career from engineering to finance and climbed another ladder. My career progressed rapidly and over a few short years I went from sales to sales management to vice president and then president of a major investment firm.

The president position was in a new city so I was parachuted into an office where there were four other vice presidents that all thought they should have had the job. Up to this point I never had a drinking problem and felt I could drink with the best of them.

When I was made president, I had a big fancy corporate office and a very big salary to match. However, I didn't know what to do because all these guys hated me even before they knew me, and the 'little Tommy' within me couldn't handle it. I began taking medication prescribed by my doctor to calm my nervousness and help me sleep. But the drugs made me feel weird and didn't help with the anxiety.

One day I made a life changing decision. I recalled that the way I really wanted to feel, when I was at my best, was when I had had just one or two drinks. I made a decision to stop taking the anxiety pills and just sip a little vodka and it really helped. I was 'cool' and able to fight corporate battles. I was being quoted often in the *Globe and Mail* and made the '*Who's Who in Canada*' list. Surviving in that environment was possible with alcohol. Vodka was my medication.

The rest of the story got worse and worse. My drinking started earlier and earlier in the day and the amount increased from a couple of ounces to six then eight and then a mickey a day. Within a year I was drinking two mickeys a day and still looking sober. From 1976 to 1982 I had six years of drinking as an alcoholic. Very few people other than my wife or kids knew I was an alcoholic. It was never a party or a good time. It was me trying to find that nirvana in the corporate world.

Then there was a discussion with my employers and my corporate success was being lost. The company was being put up for sale and I wasn't invited to be a part of it.

With a wife and four teenagers I was out of work and stayed the way for over a year.

I tried to quit drinking making a promise to my wife and children that I would quit. I wanted to stop and got so I didn't even like the taste of alcohol. But again and again I would drink and pass out on a chair and the couch. The family would search for and find my hidden bottles and I would wake up in shame and find the bottles piled on the kitchen table. The doctors said I was allergic to alcohol. My wife was pleading and as a husband and father I really wanted to quit.

I went to a few AA meetings and found out and admitted that I was an alcoholic. However, because of my success in life I couldn't accept that I was powerless. My attitude was, I know I've got a problem. I can solve it myself.

Prior to me entering the program I associated with no one. Outside a loving and concerned family I was absolutely alone. I had no friends and didn't want any. For more than a year, each day my wife went to her job and then I would go buy two mickeys and a bottle of wine and crackers and that was my world. I spent the days parked by a dirty little creek behind the mall and drank and fed the ducks. They were my friends. They understood me.

Then one day, I woke up in a dirty, filthy room with prison bars. I was in a suit and I didn't know how I got there. I asked a guard, how did I get here? He said, a hit and run, and he closed the door and left me there. I thought a 'hit and run' meant death. From eleven that night until seven the next morning I thought I'd killed someone. I couldn't believe that I, a person who wanted to be a good father and husband and a good community man who worked with people who were disabled, and had been written about in the paper for my good work was in this place. I thought if I was drunk and killed someone and left the scene, I was going to jail for a long time and I would rather die.

Turn's out there was no hit and run. In fact I was just found asleep in the parked car. But I've never been so terrified in my life. Very scared, I went to an AA meeting that night, and there was no looking back. I don't have any doubt that I'm an alcoholic and would not have made it without the help of a lot of very caring people and belief in a higher power.

When I had gone to AA previously, I thought that I had to admit that I was a bad and weak person. Joining AA didn't compute with me initially because to do the first step I would have to be admitting that I was bad and weak. That went against everything I had had drilled into me over a lifetime.

After a few days sober I stopped shaking and lost all desire to ever take a drink again. Early in the program one person in AA made a statement that was very helpful to this stubborn alcoholic. She allowed me to accept and know that I wasn't a bad man and I wasn't a weak man but I was a sick man and my sickness was making me do bad, weak things, and that without help I was powerless. AA literally came into my life overnight and went from something I knew nothing about to my constant guide and mentor. I couldn't get enough of it and loved every meeting I went to.

In my fourth step I looked at my upbringing. I grew up in the 1930s and 40s when it was considered okay to 'whop' a child with an ironing cord. Or you would be told, wait until your father comes home. Then he would take the belt off. I have this need to be loved and appreciated.

There is a need for me to be affirmed constantly, a need to be loved, and often reinforced.

Today I am mostly the type of person who lets things go by and avoid controversy and confrontation. I think that is helpful. My state of mind is recovered. I like to say life is still a bumpy road but now I'm wearing AA shock absorbers.

There are people that want to rewrite the *Big Book of Alcoholics Anonymous*. But I think the book and the principals that are involved in it are exactly the way it is supposed to be.

Sometimes I get to thinking that I could actually take a drink and get away with it and then go back to being a social drinker. I'm that stubborn. But, of course, that would be the huge problem because three days or three months later I would say see, I had proved it before so now I can do it again and drink. I don't want to go there. I don't ever want to risk it. There is no temptation to have a drink what so ever. The principals of AA got me sober but also gave me so much more; it is my guide to living.

You can't be married sixty years with four children and twelve grandchildren without a lot of issues. I can look to the higher power and I can usually find an answer. I steer away from talking about a personal God. I have never been able to think in terms of a personal God that makes decisions about what happens to people on an individual basis. For example as a volunteer, I work with people with very serious disability and see kids whose bodies are twisted up and have brain damage. That is not my idea of what a God would do. I don't think God decides whose house burns down and who wins the lottery. My higher power has to do with wisdom, nature, love, truth, and caring. Praying to God and hearing an answer doesn't work for me. But I believe the power of God works through people. I will go into a quiet place and, in my mind, think about a bunch of wise AA old timers and try to explain my problem as best as I can and think what would the old timers advise me to do. Then, so often I intuitively hear answers in my mind that works for me. I've been very fortunate in my life to have sixty years married to a wonderful woman. We were together a good twenty years before I became alcoholic and now more than thirty years since recovery.

I built another company after I became sober and it was successful thanks to opportunity, some hard work, some luck and the AA principles as a guide. Now we are comfortable in retirement

The steps are beautifully written and easy to misunderstand. You can't get anywhere until you admit you have a problem. That's the first step. The second step is "came to believe that God could restore me to sanity." I never went to church, how do I say I believe in God? How do you do that – because at that time I didn't believe? Step one is a step you take but step two is a process. You go to lots of meetings and you 'come' to believe over time. Also within step two it doesn't say God's going to do anything. It says came to believe that a power 'could' restore you to sanity. So many newcomers wants to read 'would' but it is 'could' – you come to believe that maybe it 'could' happen. You see this person sober and this person sober and think maybe it 'could' happen to me. So many people struggle over the semantics but it's written the right way.

The third step is made a decision to turn your life over – people want to read 'turn' your life over but it's 'made a decision' to turn. If your body is in poor shape and you make a decision to go to the gym, that does not give you muscles. It's a decision to go. It's an act. You're deciding to do that. Some people think God will just take over for you. They usually fumble around for a while and then go take a drink. Instead, what comes after that step three decision is step four and the real work begins. You need to grab some paper and get on with step four.

I admit that, even after all this time, I still need this affirmation. Little Tommy still needs to hear people say, your okay, your a good guy.

I've made it into my 80's now and I'm full of gratitude. I've had a really interesting life.

I have thirty-three years of sobriety and planning lots more yet.

John – 34 years

When I was five years old I moved with my parents to a new province and began school. I was a momma's boy, the youngest of three brothers and two sisters. My closest sister was ten years older and my oldest brother was twenty years older. There was one brother that passed away before I was born. He would have been nineteen years older. Apparently I could say the name of my closest sister before I could say my mother's name.

In kindergarten the teacher had a very shrill voice. I was afraid to go to the bathroom, and I peed myself, and the person beside me got blamed. I remember the teacher wacked a girl's hand with scissors. I never did well in school unless I repeated a grade and I did it twice. In those days there was corporal punishment; a teacher banged this child's head against the wall and pushed him down the stairs. I can still see that like it was yesterday, and this teacher was a good, church-going guy. Everyday someone was being nailed. There was a lot of fear in me at school.

High school, it was a bit better. I didn't get the best grades. When I went to counseling, I said my grades were not good and that my mind had a tendency to wander. When I was sixty I realized that I had attention deficit; it helped fill in the puzzle.

When I drank, I was a clown. The second year in grade nine I started drinking. I worked after school part-time from five until nine. They gave me an adult job. I was seventeen or eighteen at the time and I was making the same wage as the adults. At home I felt that I was more or less seen and not heard. My parents were poor.

The older guys that worked at the factory, they asked me to go hunting. They were twenty-six or twenty-seven, and it felt good just to be accepted. After hunting they took me to a pub, but I said I was not old enough because I was seventeen at the time. I had eight to ten drafts of beer and I didn't black out. I felt like I belonged.

I laughed at the jokes, made some comments, it was a good time. If drinking had stayed like that, I would still be drinking.

From then on, if I was not drinking I would be thinking of drinking. When there was conflict at work with the boss or someone, I knew, I would drink. But I would drink if things were good or bad or normal. I got in conflict at work. There was an impaired driving charge. They were heavy drinkers at the place I worked. They had families, too. I applied for a service-training job, went for training, and transferred to another city. I had lost my driver's license, and it was supposed to come back, but it was late coming back in the mail. They found out at my job. Other people took me out for service calls. There were times they didn't take me back to the shop instead they would take me home because we were drinking. It was a hush-hush job, meaning people didn't talk about the drinking on the job. They would go back to work with fishing rods. Everything was in good working order and nothing was breaking down because everything was new as it was only opened for three years. It was a good time. There was a place in Walkerton that I would drive to for a milkshake and it would be a fourteen-mile drive. I left to get it for my coffee break, which would start when I got back.

It was a good job, but they felt they were short-changed because I didn't have a license. That job was not a good fit. I got a job at the gas company as a gas service man and worked there for thirty years. I started drinking there, too. I transferred to gas measurement and set up for installation on site. I didn't have to be on call any more. The last years, from 1981 until 1999, I was a sober person. I got to the point where in my drinking things were not working out.

When I got into a relationship I thought we would be best friends. There was a woman who was married that I was seeing, and she had an abortion. That bothered me. That was her third pregnancy in a year. It really upset me, and I started to drink a lot then. It got to a point that I didn't want to get out of bed in the morning.

I bottomed out when my sister phoned me and said how are you doing? I said if I could get off the sofa I would probably shoot myself. A friend had brought over some nerve pills that flattened me. My sister said she was going to call my brothers. One of them was in the program. At that point he was sober a few years today he has been for abstinent for thirty-eight years. My brother called the doctor and they took me to the hospital. The doctor asked me if I had a drinking problem. I said that is quite obvious.

I thought they would take me to the psychiatric ward. However, they took me to the detoxification unit. I couldn't stand the detox. They put me in the holding room and I said I'm out of here. I was told that if I left for longer than twenty minutes, then they would discharge me. I went home. My brothers were there cleaning up my place, and they were surprised to see me back. They took me to a meeting. At the meeting the people welcomed me even though I was hung over and drunk. There was a person who welcomed me. He had a calm voice and steady hand. I developed that calm voice and steady hand.

I've had two relationships in the program and they both ended. It was troublesome for me. They both had been married before. I felt destitute again, my brother saw that I was having some problems, and he said, John, that happens a lot when you get involved in relationships with people in the program.

So I dated outside the program and I kept trying. I went on a blind date to install a gas dryer and that was how I met my wife in 1992. We hit it off. She had good friends and morals and liked to ski and was a normal person. It was a bit slow at first, but we began dating and then we moved in together.

In the meantime her sister died, and we ended up with the kids. I had put my house up for sale. The day her sister was diagnosed with bone cancer I would have stayed in my own house but the house was sold. I knew from previous relationships that baggage made it difficult to have relationships. I had no dependents and my house was paid for. If my house was not sold I would have stayed in my own house, by myself when her sister died.

We moved into the sister's house because the husband wasn't able to take care of things and there were no nurses until the last month of her life. She was horribly sick. She just had to roll over and would break a bone. The daughter was seventeen and not very nice to her mother. For example one day the daughter was looking for a CD. The mother was hospitalized at home.

The mother said I'm sorry I haven't seen it. The daughter said, how would you know, you can't even walk. My wife said, watch your manners. The daughter had her issues.

When my wife's sister died. Her husband fell to pieces and went to grief counseling and met another woman who was a recent widow. They were each other's Tylenol and aspirin, but they did not have any common interests or intimacy. The kids didn't go for it, and the kids moved in with us for a cooling-off period. Then the father said, you can have them, and he never supported them.

We had moved into a condo. The grandmother was well off, not rich, but the grandmother died and then the daughter got her car. We moved into my wife's mother's house. We had to widen the driveway so we could park all the cars. There was no appreciation of anything we did. I didn't know where to go because I didn't have my place. So there was no place to run. This all happened in sobriety. We still have the boy living with us. The girl got married. The boy, who is now a man, says he has it tougher than me getting a job. I said, the kids across the street have jobs and they are younger than you. There are counselors next door who have jobs. What is wrong with you? He wanted to apply for social assistance. He dropped out of college and he pretended he was going. My wife didn't want to lay the hammer down, thinking he would go back to his father's. So that situation was a bit trying to deal with in sobriety but we made it through.

I took up downhill skiing when I was in sobriety with another person in the program, and it gave me some common interests. A lot of people do not do anything. They have coffee and a lot of time it is just gossip about other people. When I retired shortly after I got a job at a recreation center and I took a part-time job driving.

Currently I am being checked out for cancer and going for further tests again. Whatever happens in life, I don't think about drinking. Every once in awhile my wife pours a glass of wine, I might smell it. As of now I'm thirty-four-and-a-half years with no desire to drink. Sometimes I have a fleeting thought of using drugs, but I like being of clear mind.

We are going for a driving holiday to South Carolina. It is very nice. We will check out places to go next spring. We had been going to a lot of all-inclusive trips to Mexico and Cuba. We did a nice trip to Alaska and sailed to Vancouver. Down the road we may go to the Mediterranean on a cruise, but first things first. We have responsibilities and that comes first. Then we play.

When I first joined AA the last thing on my mind was the steps. I was just glad to be detoxified. I didn't start working the steps until well into two years. There was a mini-step four and five when a relationship broke up and I was struggling a bit. A woman in the program and she said have you ever done a fourth or fifth step? I did a step on how it was affecting me. At the time I was doing good things to get favours, sexual intimacy, and other things. The fifth step I did with my first sponsor; I just blurted out things that I would never tell anyone. He looked at me, shocked, and I said I never did those things anymore.

Now, knowing the steps, I was afraid of the fifth step. But the fear was out of context. Anything that comes up now I can say to anyone. It wasn't until I was about seven years sober, and I heard about the Joe and Charlie tapes that it clicked, and there were a lot of *AA Big Book* study groups. There was an outline for completing the steps but I never did go through the steps until I met a man in AA and we joined a study group. That was when I did the fourth step, but

I never really did a step with anyone until the fifth step. I was about seven years sober, and then I did step eight, making a list of people I had harmed, but I never sat down and made a list. A person in AA said you know whom you have hurt and by being sober and by being a more caring and decent person you are making amends. People look up to me now. On my tenth anniversary, they had a big party. I was recognized and I felt appreciated. As far as the ninth, it was something completed throughout my sobriety. There are people, who I have been harsh with, so I said, I'm sorry I was harsh with you. That was not a proper way to respond. In most cases they shrugged it off. Deep down inside, I think I gained respect from them.

Step ten I do a lot – to take a personal inventory, and when wrong promptly admit it. I review and say my prayers at night and thank God for a good day and say, please bless my friend and comfort the sick.

I used to put myself first. Now I put myself in the position of those who were sick. I'm still trying to improve and think of other people and say a prayer to please assist them and bless them and give them a good night's sleep and give them a hug.

With step ten I continue to try to maintain emotional balance under all conditions. I'm getting tired of whipping myself. My sponsor, sponsees, and friends, they think that I'm a good guy. My sister-in-law said, you are the best thing that ever happened to my wife.

Step eleven goes, "sought through prayer and mediation to improve our conscious contact with God as we understood him, praying only for knowledge of his will for us and the power to carry that out." In my prayers I don't ask for knowledge of his will for me, I say please help them if you can. I know that when I have a good day, it's not just my good day it's a good day for everyone one around me. I try just to be a good person. What I want to be depends on my attitude and expectations and how selfish my entitlements are. That's my inventory right there.

Step twelve is carrying the message to the person who still suffers. The steps, they are there; it depend how you want to do them.

My first sponsor said, do the golden rule and do unto others as you want to be done unto. How should a person live his life? I like living the golden rule. When you die someone is going to give you a eulogy. A lot of times the person they are doing the eulogy for, they will talk about every good thing the deceased person had done. The final outcome of the conversation is to live your life in such a ways that when they give your eulogy the preacher doesn't have to lie. In this program we have a chance to clean up our lives, to live sober and walk sober, make amends and to be decent people. The program has helped me to live the golden rule.

I try not to judge people and to think too much. The answers will come when they are supposed to come to me. How is life now? It's not perfect but I have a wonderful house; it is a nice bungalow. There is a non-profit house next door and we help to take care of it. I put in four gardens for them. We have a nice garden; we have a pleasant neighbourhood, not the best but really good neighbours. Some wonder why I am putting in gardens. Doing this helps me. I have a giving personality. I look at the ulterior motivation, that the garden befits the community. My back yard is like a forest, and that's why I'm taking care of the property next year. The Director gives me freedom – I want to make there place a flagship. It's going to be a nice garden. I also volunteered at the women's prison, doing a group and now and I will be a driver for them.

When I got into the program I remembered how sick I was, and I still remember how sick I was, and seeing relapses that keep me away from a drink. I just had enough. I was sick and tired, and I found out that I could have a lot more fun without becoming a hazard to myself, or anyone around me. My definition of alcoholism is that when it becomes a hazard to anyone around me.

Paul – 20 years

My dry date is Dec 2, 1995. It is my second dry date. The first dry date was January 19, 1994. My main drug of choice is alcohol, although in my early teens I started with pot, THC, hash and a little bit of alcohol. I was able to get drugs easier than alcohol because my friend knew people in their early 20s. Also, my siblings smoked, and I was able to steal from them, and I also stole alcohol. I grew up in a house with strict regulations and rules about how you are supposed to be.

We emigrated from Glasgow in the mid-1960s to escape poverty. I was five, and I do not remember Scotland at all. I remember Canada. From the time I was six until ten or eleven I received many mixed messages about what to do, but they did not apply to everyone in the family equally, and it didn't apply to my parents, particularly my father, who was an alcoholic. We had Scottish friends over to the house they had emigrated from Scotland too. My father's drinking progressed over time. It started on weekends, and then progressed to through the week.

He started to miss a significant amount of work. The reason I'm saying this is that I'm not blaming alcoholism on my parents, but I started to experience it when I was a child. I would see my dad's drinking and my neighbours would see it. He was at soccer games, and people would know he was drunk because he was falling over. People would say, look at that guy.

As a child of that guy, I felt a lot of shame because he would fall over. I didn't know what to do with the shame. I had no words to know what shame was. It was only when I was in recovery that I knew what shame was, and Adult Children Of Alcoholics helped. At ten, I did not know that my mother also felt shame. She didn't want to talk about it. We just didn't talk about it.

As I grew and got older, at twelve or thirteen, my mother started to drink a lot. It was almost as if she gave up. She couldn't tolerate alcohol, and she became drunk very fast. The arguments were tremendous. Now we experienced verbal violence. It felt unsafe. I didn't know what to expect; you couldn't invite any friends over. I became very keenly aware of people around me in order to feel safe. I needed to know how to feel secure. I became acutely aware of how I felt, almost on guard, very, very, hypervigilant, unbelievably vigilant. Emotionally, I would scan the house. I used to go in the side door. It had the stairs going downstairs and upstairs, so I could have a very good idea of what was going on. It was crazy. I had three brothers. The two older brothers and two older sisters were gone, so I felt I had to protect my younger brother. He was involved in hockey.

Between grades seven and eight, things went downhill. There was lots of stuff happening in the house. I got introduced to some new people on our street, and they gave us hash and pot. It was the summer, and I started to use pot between grade seven and eight. I didn't think of any consequences.

The summer I started drinking I drank just like my father. I had some homemade wine from someone's basement, and I was out of control and couldn't walk. With the pot, I felt so much different, and within a week or two of using it I got high and all of my problems and all of the things I was feeling, all of the insecurity, everything was gone. That was the downfall. I felt like, I'm at home I'm safe.

In grade seven and eight I got good at rolling pot, and then my friends, they liked to smoke it too. So I found someone who would sell to me on credit, and it was fifty-five dollars for an ounce and I would sell three-quarters for fifteen each or twenty dollars each, and I would smoke for free. That way I would always have the stuff. I became very clearly addicted, and started to smoke it during the summer and was stoned all day in the summer of grade seven and eight. That summer was a right off. Then I pulled it back a bit.

At the same time my parents were continuing to drink. I smoked drugs on the weekend. I didn't smoke it at school because I didn't want to get caught. In the summer of grade eight and nine, that was when my alcoholism started. I would use a bit of alcohol and pot, acting almost like my own pharmacist. Selling drugs continued, I started going downtown and was becoming popular dealing. Then I began drinking more, and I became like my dad and would be inebriated and slobbery and fall. Someone said that I could not drink alcohol because I was tired and that I needed some amphetamines. Then I began smoking pot, doing bennies, and drinking. So because of my connections, I sold pharmaceutical bennies. I became almost like a little drug dealer, and that went on for nearly two years.

In grade nine I totally lost control, and failed five credits out of nine and couldn't think clearly. The next five years I had to make up all the credits I lost in grade nine, so I started to pull it back on the drugs and alcohol use over the next few years. For the next few years I tried to control it, and when I couldn't control it bad things would happen. I would break something or say something bad.

At the same time, my dad and mom continued to drink. They would go to hockey tournaments, and I wouldn't go. I became popular because I had parties in my basement. I knew I wanted to go to university, and when it became time my parents didn't support it. They had no money. So I started working for my dad, doing drywall and plaster. By the time of grade twelve I totaled my dad's car. My pot smoking was crazy. I was very unhappy that I was not going to university.

My first high school girlfriend broke up with me because of my drinking. I was crushed. One day I was drinking and smoking pot in the basement and watched a show on drug abuse, and I said, that is me.

I'm an alcoholic they are talking about me. I'm a drug addict they are talking about me. I was seeing a counselor because of the things that were happening at the time. They asked me about my drug and alcohol use, and I didn't tell them. Later I went to an addiction counselor in the basement of a mall, and I told him my story.

I was low, my hair was long, I was out of control. They told me I should stop and I went to AA. Realizing that every time I was in trouble I was always pissed. I quit everything. It was March of 1983. There was a guy in AA, he went to the good morning group, and there were a couple of streetwise guys there, and they said, are you going to be sober or sober and smoking pot?

We don't care, you still get your medallion. This is what happened, I got my first-year medallion in Jan 22, 1985, but I was twenty-two months clean from alcohol but only twelve months clean from drugs.

To me it was miraculous. My high school career was a disaster, but what happened to me was miraculous. In 1985 I met all of these young people in recovery that were positive and young like me, in their early twenties. I was twenty-two in 1985, I was twenty-one when I got my first medallion. I met six or seven young people that all came to AA at the same time. I realized that I had a pot problem and amphetamine problem. So I did not always feel comfortable in AA, we ended up starting a Narcotics Anonymous meeting in our area. At the time I backed off on the AA stuff. Some of the people I met in the program were going to school and I still wanted to go to University. I took a one-year diploma program and met my sponsor.

My girlfriend and I had a daughter, and she baby died. I had a lot of grief, and I started to smoke pot again. Then I stopped going to meetings. I said, I'm okay I'm just going to smoke, and then my sponsor began to do cocaine and to sell, and it was good and pure. It triggered my amphetamine craving. I felt like, oh my God, this is it. I found the thing that makes me feel good. I stopped smoking pot and was doing cocaine and did that for a little over a year.

Then I stopped it when there was a bust at the house I was living in.

I was feeling like a hypocrite with everything that I learned, and my spirituality and my connection to God all that stuff slid away. I got married, and I had another daughter, and my wife was giving me a hard time. My parents continued to drink and were chronic alcoholics. It got worse, and worse, and worse, and finally I cleaned it all up. I met a priest and stayed at his house and was working in construction and returned to college. This priest said, why don't you become a counselor rather than working in construction? I did a two-year diploma and finished that.

My parents were still drinking, and I was still married. She didn't like that I didn't drink, because she wanted to have fun. I finished my diploma in 1992 and then realized that I wanted to teach in schools or be a guidance counselor, so I was back on track. Then I realized that to be a teacher you need a degree, so I went back to university. That took another two years.

Then my mom died in 1992, and I was completely devastated, and my dad hit the bottle hard. There was stuff going on in my brain and I was thinking, am I an alcoholic? Then one day in my last year of school, just after my mom died, someone ordered some beer and he asked me, do you want one? I drank it, and as soon as it touched my lips I had that feeling and craving for alcohol, and I said to myself, do I have enough money to get really drunk, and I did. The guy I was with said, you look like you liked that. That relapse lasted three years. I was drinking and losing control and getting into fights with my wife. I had a job at a treatment hospital, and I had to keep my drinking under wraps.

I got into a huge fight with my wife and was having a custody issue with my daughter. In 1995 it all blew up, the shit hit the fan when I got home. She said, I'm going to call and get you arrested, I'm going to leave you, and take the house, or you need to call this counselor in one hour. Then I thought, I'm going to lose everything. Then I thought, oh my God, that is true, everything they said in AA, and I phoned the counselor. The counselor told me, you should go back to AA or NA.

That would cause problems at work because you have to be sober so many years before you can work there. I had to tell them at work that I had been drinking, and it got out of control, and I didn't get into any trouble. It was very emotional when I went into work and told them that I was an alcoholic. They sent me to a doctor, and the doctor said yes, you need treatment, so I went for seven weeks.

So since December 2, 1995, I've been sober, and I went back to AA meetings. I didn't go back to NA. I heard it was very chaotic, and there was not a lot of sobriety there. The solid structure at AA was what I needed. I also went for aftercare for three years once a week. I found a new sponsor, found guys around my age in recovery, and started to do the steps again.

During this time I realized I shouldn't be married. We didn't love each other we were just married. My focus was on recovery, and I realized I could never safely drink and I can never safely use again. That realization is the biggest difference from the other times before. I didn't want to accept it, but when I picked up a drink I began where I left off before I became abstinent. Attending maybe six hundred meetings a year, two meetings a day, I got re-engaged in recovery for lots of good reasons.

The honest truth is the steps are what saved my life. First of all, I always had a *Twelve and Twelve*, and I had always read that those who are engaged in the steps were successful. The first line of step one is, "who cares to admit defeat," it was like a hand hit me on the head and said, look at you. At nineteen you were here and it took you another seven or eight years to admit it.

I had liked the feeling of getting high, but I didn't like the aftereffects. It became a question of can I use and not get the consequences, if I only drank wine or if I only smoked a little pot? It was craziness. I didn't accept step one—who cares to admit complete defeat, and that my life was unmanageable. It was simple to admit my life was unmanageable. I just had to make a checklist—criminal charge, almost lost my wife, my daughter, my home, and my job.

With step two—came to believe that a power greater than yourself could restore me to sanity. That was simple I knew the power.

Step three was more difficult. It involved the action of giving up control. I always felt there would be the black hole of nothingness if I gave over my power to God. There was a lot of time spent asking old timers what they thought, and sharing it. I kept reading and connecting it to my Roman Catholic faith, where God is a powerful, revengeful God. I had to work through some of that stuff related to my past religious beliefs. It was a decision. Acronyms related to God did not work for me. I knew it was God. I know it works. I also had a good sponsor at this time.

When it came to step number four I took out *The Big Book of Alcoholics Anonymous* and took out the *Twelve and Twelve* and took out the chart and made a list of everything, all the stuff I could remember. I did it exactly how they said it. Listing fears and exactly how they said to do it, including writing about relationships too. I had ten or twelve pages.

At the same time, I was continuing to see a physician for treatment. I called my sponsor and spent three or four hours going through the fourth and fifth. Then I did the sixth and seventh steps. It was simple—ask him to remove my shortcomings. Reading *The Big Book* and the *Twelve and Twelve* and learning how they go through it was still something I did regularly. Reading was good as I was very cerebral and intellectual. I started to make amends where I could. Some people did not want anything to do with me. Most didn't even remember the thing I did.

Step ten, eleven, and twelve, it is just a connection of the first nine steps. I continued to keep a personal inventory and started meditating again and living a different way. I went back to church, looking for fulfillment through the spiritual principles. There was a realization that life is about people and connection, not about the money you have and how much security you have.

It's always a struggle when things are not going great in my new marriage or work. Those situations still pull my little strings of self-centeredness, and I would think, is this really God's will or a bunch of garbage that is happening to me? I've come to believe that things come about just because people are people.

It's about taking responsibility after what happens. A classic example is when I lost a job because they were cutting costs, and I thought, oh my God, what is happening? I don't think that God meant for that to happen. I had moved my family for the job. So I started my own business, and now I have clients and my children are in a good community. My children are in smaller classrooms and that works out well, and my daughter has found a good soccer coach. God makes good things out of what happens. What can I do to make it happen? When one door closes then three windows open. I'm ready to act; it is doing his will. We have a path that we travel. I don't know if the gospel is all valid and he knows everything. I just have to have faith that everything is going to happen for the good.

Alcoholism got in the way of who I was supposed to be. Recovery made me the person I was supposed to be. I'm in my twentieth year of recovery. It all started with step one and quitting. I'm connected to a spiritual life, and I'm just asking myself what I am supposed to do.

I'm human, and old thinking can creep in, and I sometimes think I would be better if I had this or that. We are built to feel good. I've had bad relationships and issues with women my whole life. I've had issues with sex, and sex was just as good as a drug. The feeling of being connected to a woman - I confused it all. I had no guidepost to tell me. My parents were alcoholic, and they were lost. It was like I re-parented myself, and it's ongoing.

I always have issues of monitoring excessiveness, like golfing or eating. If one thing is good, a thousand is better. Addiction is not just about substance it's about the brain being caressed with enjoyable feelings. I need to be careful with how much coffee or sugar I use.

Working with others is important. I'm sponsoring a couple of guys, but what I have found is that my true passion is working with people who want to get recovery. Fortunately, that is my job, it is my twelve-step work, and that clearly kept me focused and connected to the program. Truly it is influential in long-term sobriety. The steps, a sponsor, staying connected to others, working with others, are all important.

My recreation before when I was drinking and drugging was going to the pubs and playing darts in a league, going to a lot of parties, and hanging out at the houses where people were drinking. In recovery I've completely changed my whole social network. I don't go to darts, the people there are there to play darts and to drink. I started playing golf, coaching soccer, and refereeing hockey. I have to work recovery in my new recreational activities. After sports events some people would drink in the car. I felt uncomfortable, so I brought my own pop and made sure I was safe. When I say to my wife, I need to go, there are no questions asked.

A lot of times I will get prepared and I would get an intuition, a connection to God. It prepares me to be careful because there might be alcohol there. I don't get parked behind a car where there is another car, and I let people know where I am going to be. I don't do recreational activities where the activity is the vehicle for drinking.

Family triggers a lot of stuff. I'm at the age where I'm a parent of children who are at the age when I started using drugs. Now my daughter is fourteen and going into grade nine. My recovery has allowed them to have a stable household, which changes the cycle of addiction. This is not just about me it's about their family and what their family will have. Our family history can change moving forward.

Diane – 34 years

I grew up surrounded by alcoholism. While there was extended family that did not drink, my family socialized mainly with families whose parents drank. A stepfather who, was very violent and abusive, and his mother, who was also an alcoholic, raised my father. On my mother's side her mother was schizophrenic and was hospitalized permanently when my mother was nine, and my maternal grandfather was an alcoholic. So others people sometimes raised both my mother and father. When my mother got pregnant at eighteen my parents married. My father was nineteen. Neither one of them had parental role models that were helpful to providing a loving, stable home. However, they tried.

From a review of my ancestry, it appears this pattern of historical trauma was passed down through the generations. One broken set of parents to their children and so forth.

My father wanted to be a minister but was pulled out of school to work on the farm when he was in grade four. He was a hard worker and did not drink or smoke. My mother an only child, raised primarily without a family and who wanted to be a mother, only worked outside the home when she needed too. In the early years, in the morning I would wake up early to have coffee with my father before he went to work. My mother made excellent pastry and took an interest in my schooling, and together they created a comfortable, though modest home where all material needs were taken care of.

At one point my father was given the opportunity to take on a new job. The employees and owners drank after work regularly. This combined with my parental grandparents moving beside us created a post-traumatic stress situation, and my father fell apart, drinking and becoming easily triggered into horrifying acts of violence directed at my mother and siblings.

My mother at this time had three children and an absence of extended family support. I hid from my father, walked on my tippy toes, and by today's standards would have shown obvious signs of mental health issues. Time, however, was interspersed with happy memories of birthday parties, friends, visiting with cousins, belief in God, and enjoyment of church and associated social functions. I attended church on my own and I received pleasure from school assignments, friends, and sports.

However, there came a day when something inside me broke. It was a tipping point of events, which broke my spirit. I felt hopeless and tried the only thing I felt was left to try as a means of being happy: alcohol. At thirteen, I drank so much I made an absolute fool of myself. The next day, regardless of the feeling of humiliation, the sense of release and freedom from suffering was greater, and a pattern of almost daily drinking began. It was never difficult for me to find something to drink either from home or someone would buy it for me. Quickly I added any drug in pill form, or smoking pot or hash; basically whatever I could access. My grades dropped, and I was kicked out of school in grade nine from three different schools. Delinquency resulted in charges in the criminal justice system and a night in jail. The crowd I associated with changed, and I associated with a violent crowd who were involved in organized crime. I also sold drugs. For a period of seven years, I continued this path, never expecting to see the age of twenty-five.

One night my aunt said she was praying for me. This was somewhat of a wake-up call, as I felt that it was an indication that something was wrong with me. Shortly after that, I had a dream that I was driving a car drunk on the way to a church, and God spoke to me in the dream, saying I was not going to make it. The car smashed and I was instantly awake in bed sitting up staring wide-eyed. The dream was so vivid, and the road I was driving on in the dream was one I often drove on drunk.

Right then and there I made a decision to quit drinking and drugs. At that time, I was about eighteen or nineteen. However, I had been drinking heavily and taking pills and smoking every night for years. I began to experience hallucinations. Terrified, I prayed for God to help me, and instantly I was out of my body, being guided by a spirit whom I believed to be Jesus; he was pure light, and no words can describe the sense of peace I felt. I quickly realized I was dying. No, I don't want to die, I said. Instantly I was back in my body, experiencing the terrifying hallucinations. Dying during withdraw is one of the reasons that Detoxification treatment programs were established. Research suggests that ten percent of individuals experience a spiritual experience in their lifetime. I feel blessed to have had this experience.

It took several attempts to quit drinking after that. It was not easy. I would try but without any awareness of why, I would begin drinking and using drugs again. Life continued to go downhill, and I continued to attempt to quit drinking. My mental health became increasingly impaired. I lost my job and I lost control over my life. Desperate, I went to the doctor to seek help. I was put on Antabuse and mood-altering drugs, including Valium. The effect of the prescription drugs on my mental health was significant. Antabuse is a drug that will make you violently sick if you drink on it and it could kill you; such was my desperation that I was willing to go to this length to quit.

At a party, someone gave me a drink, telling me it was water but it was alcohol. Quickly,

I became very ill and ended up in the hospital, in the Detoxification Centre. It was a non-medical Detoxification Unit, and all I received for the withdrawals was L-Tryptophan. The hallucinations were again part of my withdrawal.

Alcoholics Anonymous was part of the Detoxification treatment, and I remembered at my first meeting having the feeling that it was now possible to anything. That did not make the withdrawal easy. At one point during withdrawal I wanted to kill myself. However, that day my brother had come to give me something, and while I cried the whole day I lived that day for him, as a woman at an AA meeting told me she lived for her family when she couldn't live for herself.

The other thing that AA taught me was that it was important to help others, so with a couple of days of sobriety I realized I had a couple of days more than the person just walking in the door, and I began reaching out to others. I tried to bring some of my relatives into the program. My father quit drinking for six months because he blamed himself for my drinking. While he returned to drinking, losing a significant amount throughout his life, he ended up dying a sober man who helped others.

After detoxification I continued to go to AA meetings regularly and was very involved, helping set up meetings, making sandwiches, cleaning up, assuming service roles, and greeting newcomers. As a young woman, I was able to help and reach out to other young women. I strictly followed what I was advised to do: getting a sponsor, completing the steps, not making any serious decisions or changes for a year, sponsoring others, not becoming involved in a relationship for a year, and was cautious for five years about making changes. AA literature was always in my purse, and I read it religiously.

At six months sober, the desire to drink was still very strong, so I prayed that it be removed, and it was instantly, and I never felt a desire to drink again. That did not mean that life was easy, it was not, but it was easier than it was when I was drinking and using. I was very committed to my sobriety and would say to others, and myself, come hell or high water, I am not going to drink. It was a mindset that was important because drinking was not an option.

After I quit drinking I was a conversational cripple. I didn't have any idea what to talk to people about. Additionally, I was now very shy. My old employer offered my job back, feeling that it might help his son to be witness to my change. Life was simple in early recovery it revolved around AA meetings, work, and exercise.

When I went to the Detoxification Centre, I removed myself from my friends and the environment I was in and began to build a new network at meetings. During my stay at Detox I found another place to live and did not communicate to anyone I associated with where I was going. Not even the man I was seeing, who was in jail at the time, knew where I went. I was just as tired of the lifestyle as I was of alcohol. It is my belief that the desire to leave the lifestyle at the same time helped me a great deal to maintain abstinence.

After one year I did all the things I had been dreaming of. I needed to rehabilitate myself and was involved in vocational rehabilitation. I went back to school, initially taking a math refresher course for grades four to eight. After completion of this, I returned to an adult high school and completed grade twelve. From there I did a B.A., an M.A., and began my Ph.D. studies. While I enjoyed academic studies, I felt that it did interfere with my relationships, as I was always busy with school.

Relationship development was definitely something else that needed to be addressed. I attended Adult Children of Alcoholics meetings, and also went to counseling, on three separate occasions to deal with issues associate to my childhood; Spending a total of about three years in counseling and group therapy. I realized that if I did not attend counseling it was unlikely I would ever have a successful relationship.

Early in my life, I had learned that the best way to avoid pain was to avoid people. Through counseling, the blackout years of my childhood came back, and I remember crying for a full two days. After the grief was anger, followed by forgiveness, acceptance, and taking responsibility for who I am today. There was a process of re-parenting myself. After that healing process I can still remember the first time I felt the presence of a person. Before that, I had built up such a strong protective shell that rarely did I even allow people to touch me. AA helped with the comfort of touching somewhat with the handshakes. Initially I did not like to hug at all and handshakes were a stretch but over time I became more comfortable with touch. Today I freely give hugs and shake hands and am comfortable in social relationships.

Intimate relationships still require a great deal of development. Working on relationships and improving my skills in this area has been an ongoing area of growth throughout my entire sobriety, which is approaching thirty-five years.

Another issue that I felt was important to address was my perception of myself. I thought that I was stupid, ugly, and fat. The reality is that I tested at an IQ of 140. I was attractive enough to catch the attention of the men I desired, and was a size six. Addressing my self-esteem was a multi-step process. Through counseling, I was asked who was the voice that was telling me I was stupid, ugly, and fat. I felt the message had come somehow through my father.

The counselor told me that the next time I heard that voice to tell it to shut up, and that helped.

The other thing I did was to become more mindful of the people I was around, and began to associate with individuals who treated me well. I began to eliminate from my life people who I did not think treated me well, and purposely associated with individuals who were kind to me.

Recreation was an area that I worked on. Most of my youth had been spent in the bars or parties, so I was unfamiliar with what to do with myself or what I liked outside of AA. Exercise, weight lifting, aerobics, and cycling were vitally important, and I sometimes spent up to three hours a day doing these activities. Outside of exercise, meeting and socializing with new AA friends was very special. There was a shared bond. I have fond memories of those days and feel the friendships made were extraordinary.

I made a list of things I thought of doing and began to go down the list to understand what I enjoyed. I found that I liked golfing lessons and the driving range, but was not keen on playing eighteen holes of golf. With the help of a great teacher, I took art lessons for a year and a half. Then I took dance lessons. Little by little I continued to go through the list, doing all the things I ever wanted to do. Still to this day I have a wish lists for things I would like to achieve.

Treating undiagnosed mental health issues was also something that came up for me to address. I was treated for a minor eating disorder and minor depression. Especially early in sobriety I would binge eat; I found this was sometimes triggered by past memories. I received six months of outpatient counseling for this but was in counseling on and off for several years. Deserts and chocolate cannot be kept in my home. Within twenty-four hours they would be gone.

Depression was mainly kept at bay through exercise, however; I found that there were periods of times where I needed brief use of anti-depressants. Once, it was when I was experiencing post traumatic stress due to working in front-line counseling for mental health issues and also working for a boss who often berated staff for no reason. I took medication for three months until I could get into a better work environment. Another period of difficulty was my menopausal years, which required two years of anti-depressants until I went back to lifting weights and doing cardio. I also have a diagnosis of attention deficit that I have found ways to manage without medication particularly through cueing, routine, and having project-based work.

Emotional intelligence has always been an issue. At first, I had to be taught how to recognize my emotions and express them appropriately. This was something I have to revisit throughout my life and continually work on. I have children, and the stress of parenting as well as having to learn how to parent was difficult. I used a lot of parenting books and trial and error. Learning to apologize was taught through AA but I often needed to revisit the concept.

For a period I stopped going to meetings. At the time I worked in the mental health and addiction system, was married to a person from AA, and later became a single mother to a child actively involved in sports. So these things justified my absence from meetings. I believe the years spent without the fellowship was a mistake because I lost the principles and support I needed to deal with the stress of everyday life.

I also found that once I quit drinking I became addicted to overeating sweets, and that my body was sensitive to food; I did better on a diet low in sugar, salt, caffeine, chocolate, and processed foods. Today I eat mainly unprocessed and organic foods when possible. Juicing has helped at times to enhance my energy.

Faith was important for me and has always been a big source of strength. The *Big Book of Alcoholics Anonymous* outlined my favourite spiritual practice, the 12 steps, which provided the best living philosophy I have found. Other than that, I found strength in non-denominational spiritual practices, reading, and meditations. The environment, particularly water sources, and trees were wonderful places for me to feel at peace and seek strength.

Early in sobriety, I had to deal with relationship issues through counseling. At times, I referred to men as being my favourite mood-altering drug. There was often a lack of wisdom in my choices. Although I went to counseling for this, it is an area of continued development. Often there are periods of time when work is prioritized over relationships, and I can work excessively, particularly as I feel I am more successful at work than relationships. I do, however, have many long-standing relationships with friends, and was able to maintain a fourteen-year marriage.

My career was successful and I achieved many goals that I had for myself. Building a network of people was a key to having a satisfying career and lots of opportunity. One of my struggles at work was my intolerance for relationships and low tolerance for unhappiness. I mainly worked on projects, which was an early career choice, and never worked in a work environment beyond three years. The work that I focused on for the majority of my career was addictions and mental health.

Today I live with my two sons and dog. I have started my own business and I love what I do. Having children helped me to have a relatively stable life and I've lived in the same house for eleven years. Exercise continues to be a part of my life, and I try to eat well, maintain a daily spiritual practice and help others. I am content with simple things and grateful for AA and the life it provided me. I often feel that the experience of being an alcoholic led me to spiritual practices, which saved my life through living the steps. The friendships I built in AA were and are very important to me, and some of the same people who greeted me at the door are still there doing the same, greeting me when I enter and living a life of abstinence too. AA provided a sense of belonging that never went away, and every time I walk in the door I feel welcome. I was twenty when I quit using alcohol and drugs. I have thirty-four years of abstinence; I am certain had I not entered recovery I would not be alive today.

Mike – 39 years

I was born during the war, and my father was away, so my mother and grandmother, with very few male figures, brought me up as an only child. You could say I was spoiled. I got everything I wanted, and if I could hold my breath I got it. My lung capacity was good. They loved me.

My dad came home a war hero. There was a picture of me holding a solider doll and dressed as a solider. He was awarded the second highest medal. This is what I remember: Everything was a party. My father worked at a brewery and my grandfather a distillery. I can remember laughter and dancing, but I don't remember people drunk. All I recall is that if you drink you have a good time, and that had a lot of influence on me as I grew up.

When I was sixteen and began to sneak drinks, it felt dishonest. So I asked my dad if I could have a beer and he said yes and took me to the Polish Legion. I was seventeen or eighteen, and I started getting drunk. It was always an excellent time. I sometimes think, why did I start drinking, and I don't know why. It just felt good. I just wanted to feel happy, and I liked the attention.

I liked it among my peers, and I usually got the drunkest. By the time I was twenty I'm in a position that I have to get married. Those things can happen, and in those days, you got married. We had three children quickly. I didn't drink much with the first child. We didn't have much money.

I had to improve my lot, and I had always wanted to be a traveling salesman, so the time came, and I got a job like that. All of a sudden, I found it easy to drink. I would get drunk once in awhile before that, but once I was out on the road I started to go drinking in bars, looking sharp in my business suit. I did this for three or four nights a week, drinking heavily, then I came home and didn't drink. The story

I told myself was if I had a job where I didn't travel I wouldn't drink. A transfer came to my home area, and I was about twenty-five when I started working local. But I couldn't stay home, so I would make excuses that I had to meet clients, and I would come home drunk.

My wife began to say there was a problem. I would get in more and more trouble and started to get impaired driving charges. There were five of them in three years. That presented a lot of problems. That three-year period was the worst. My wife said we should go to counseling, so we went to see a priest, but that didn't work. My nerves were bad, so I went to see a doctor, and he asked what was wrong, and I said I had the flu and was treated for the flu. I couldn't tell the truth.

With previous charges I was put in jail for two weeks, and now I was looking at going away for six months. I was miserable and depressed, feeling a whole gamut of emotions. When I talked to the lawyer, he said, you need to get something from someone saying you need help, or you got help.

I went to outpatient counseling, and the guy would talk about when he got drunk. Well, that made sense, but the only thing he put in the letter was that I went, but the judge wanted to see that I was doing something about the problem. When the judge saw the letter he said, that is very succinct, I'm going to take away your license again, and you need to see somebody at the Addiction Research Foundation.

I said, no, I don't think I'm an alcoholic. He said, okay, let's see if you are a controlled drinker. Then he sent me to talk to a counselor, and the first thing I remember, I was asked to go to a meeting by an AA member who worked at the Police Department. He said, would you like to go to a meeting? I said, yes, I think I should. He asked, do you think you are an alcoholic? I responded, I really do not know.

Then he came and sat beside me. All the meetings I'd had before, the person was across the table. With him moving beside me, it removed the client-patient relationship. He then told me his story. I did what he said, and he became my sponsor. That was the start of it.

I went to a meeting, and the thought came to me that for once in my life I should do what people told me. So for once in my life I did what people told me. Never did I take direction before, not as a child, teen, or adult. Always wanting to do it my way.

That was the beginning of sobriety in late October 1976. It was the morning meeting. That Saturday night there was a party that we went to, and I had three beers, and they were the worst three beers I had in my life. He said, you just don't take a drink for today, and that was in my mind. Then we went to another place, and I was asked, what would you like to drink, and I said,

Nothing. It was just three drinks, and I felt so bad. After that, I didn't go to any places where people would offer me a drink. I found quitting drinking was easy. It was the living that was the hard part. That was difficult, and I think that is where AA comes into play. I could talk about why I felt uncomfortable you could talk out loud. You couldn't talk like that at a bar. I felt better.

I started hanging around people who were sober a little bit longer than me. The first time I witnessed a guy leaving in the program and drinking. I didn't know people could do that.

I couldn't figure out how I was going to get out of the problems drinking had caused. Being nearly bankrupt, everything was like a hornets' nest. I was thirty-five, married with three teenagers. I became unemployed and went through a fifteen-month period of unemployment. I couldn't buy a job. They blacklisted me. I had to start over.

Our son became a drug addict and lived on the streets. He found help from a friend who never abandoned him, who was a Jehovah Witness. He married a woman who was a long-time member of the Jehovah Witness. We went and thanked them for doing what we couldn't do.

We also went through marriages and divorces with our children. My one daughter had a brain tumor. She was operated on within two days. The doctor was able to reduce the tumor to the size of a dime. He was not able to get it all. I remember he had his back to the wall and eyes closed. He was physically exhausted and I thought, why didn't you fix her? I took her to an AA group, and she decided to dedicate her life to health care. Before going to the meeting, she was a normal teenager. She said, I think within ten years I'm going to be the director of a hospital. Wow, this was a rotten teenager. There were some repercussions from her illness, but she worked in health care and later was in charge of graduate students at the university. She ended up in a hospital. Her mental health is fragile. Now she is on long-term disability. She has a good psychiatrist that keeps her on the right medication, but every once in awhile she would need to go to the hospital.

Three years after her tumor surgery I'm at a Friday meeting, and I'm still carrying a resentment to the doctor who did the operation. Then I was introduced to his wife, who said that she and her husband prayed every night for my daughter. I thought he was so impersonal, but I was wrong, and I broke down and cried. That was one of those moments when my stupid ideas kept me in a state of non-forgiveness. I said, holy smokes, there was an example about keeping an open mind.

The all-important factor for me is going to meetings. I need to go to meetings. I remember one man who started drinking said, it's like I took the most precious thing I had and it's never come back.

The steps became a part of my life. I began a home group study with a person with long-term sobriety of five years. This was what they were doing in Windsor. The big thing was the emphasis on the fourth and fifth step, and we were not going to move on unless we all completed the fourth and fifth step. It was like pulling teeth. The day I started writing the fourth it was like I had a magic pen. I couldn't stop writing. After I had finished I went with another person, and we sat in the back of his car behind the ski hill and talked for two hours. I didn't feel elated or relieved. When I came to the AA program, it wasn't easy. There were kid problems, domestic problems, and life problems. The program has always been able to help us through.

The twelfth step can be done many, many ways, being of service to people, not just to alcoholics. I am more comfortable with the eleventh step now. Sometimes I can get into a space of being almost meditative, not on demand but particularly lying in bed when I'm not tired. I think I've got to empty my head. Sometimes I think I'm almost floating, and things are coming into my head instead of going out. The fourth and fifth steps are over rated. They are mentioned so much that they scare new people. If we would just take them in our stride, it would be easier. But people sometimes put pressure on others, saying, if you don't take your fourth and fifth step you will get drunk. When the suggestions are taken away, and you take it in stride, then it makes it easier.

Peers and role models are important. My role model today is Tom. He does everything. Being in the program allowed me to do things I couldn't before. For example, there was always a quiet fund to help people, and for once in my life I was able to help someone. Sponsors and role models, going to meetings, and doing what I'm told were important. I've had a few great experiences with sponsees and I feel good about that.

Additionally, believing in a power beyond my imagination. That power is astounding. What changes can happen when you believe in that power greater than yourself. I can't change others I can only change myself. We can have all these prayers and good thoughts, but until they are acted on we need not do the steps but live the steps. Sometimes I have trouble doing that.

I never went to treatment. I went to a few counseling centres. Some were useful, but mainly it was AA that was helpful. We hung out with AA people, and we have had the most fun with AA people. What happened was I became a father once I was sober, and not long after I became a grandfather. I found as the family grew I started to like my place. I began to like being a husband, grandfather, and father.

Now, I'm the oldest in my family. My sister is thirteen years younger. Although they are my brothers and sisters, I've never felt that close because I've been more like a father. Now I'm thinking I'm the chief. There is supposed to be wisdom with age and wisdom with long-term sobriety. Now I feel they are looking at me for that knowledge. I don't know what a grandfather is supposed to be like. My grandsons think I'm crazy, and we joke around, and I like that. Now I go to some of their sporting events.

We were on the verge of bankruptcy. Now we are in a position that we don't owe anyone anything. We are not rich, but it's a nice peaceful feeling. I never had that peaceful feeling before, as I was always worried about keeping up with other guys and who has a bigger car and TV. AA has taught me to be grateful for what I have got. I tried to do everything I was asked. Sometimes it's not about sponsoring, it's about opening up meetings. It isn't fun getting up at 5:30, in the morning, but you do it to try and help someone somehow. In the neighbourhood, one of the things I did last year was volunteer for the blues festival. It was a nice feeling. I'm involved in and enjoy history. I moderate a website. There are about 8,000 members. When I took it over there were 4,000. I have people who think I'm an expert, and they ask me questions. Somebody said, wow, Mike you tell the best stories. I enjoy people, and I can't say I enjoyed people before. The only drinking buddy I had is now dead. He was ten years older than me. I used to bring him home because then my wife could see that I was not as bad as him.

The nightmares of drinking and driving and what is going to happen next and thinking what have I done now, that is gone away.

Having one spouse helps. We can be at each other's throats, and happily the next morning she can be okay. For me, it takes a couple of days. We just put up with each other's craziness. She went for about fifteen years to Al-Anon, and she allowed me the privilege of going to meetings at night; she could have said, I need you here. I look at people who have to start over, and it puts you behind the eight ball. I give more credit to her. Like all those tragedies in life, I've learned how to handle them.

I realized that I was hanging around a bad crowd, so I gave up all my friends from the past. Only going to places if I had a fit spiritual condition or had a reason to be there. My last drink was with the ball team. If I went back to baseball I could have slipped easily, so I lost some good friends but I found lots of new ones.

Belief in a higher power is important. You can be an atheist, but you need to believe in something. It doesn't have to be a Christian deity.

I have good memories of old timers. With thirty-nine years the closer you get to the person the more flaws you see. I enjoy being around people. There are people that need more than we have to offer in AA. I can understand if someone moves on as long as they stay sober. If they don't make it, they don't give alcoholism enough credit for having a hook in them. It's a vicious disease. They misjudge it; they are in denial.

When I came into the program, I started planning my first talk and planning the first twenty-five years. I figured I would be living out on Hidden Valley Drive and have several Cadillacs. Now we are two people with four bathrooms, five phones, three flat screens. I'm just one purchase away from the happiness consumer spending will get you. Gambling is an emotional roller coaster for me, so I can't gamble

My experiences with counseling outside of AA have been mixed. We went to family counseling early on to learn how to have family meetings. Second time I didn't like counseling. I went to a woman, and she wanted to meet my wife, and they went out to dinner. It was a violation of trust. The third time I went, I saw the guy and was given a huge list of things to check off. I was going through a depression, and went through all these questionnaires and then they wanted seventy-five dollars. One time I went for an employment and stress situation and enjoyed it. Another time I got interviewed by a woman at the addiction service foundation and she was trying to pick me up. I never went back. It was two years after that that I quit. Counseling has not been a great experience. Basically I've relied on my fears, AA, and literature. Scott Peck was helpful.

Sue – 37 years

My mother told me that when they brought me home from the hospital that they took me to bed with them at night. She said that every night they had to stuff their ears with cotton batting because I cried. I think that sometimes it explains why rejection was so difficult. My mother ruled with an angry fist, and she was a dry drunk. No matter what I was feeling, it was the wrong thing to feel, so I shut down at an early age. My mother's father was an alcoholic, and she grew up in a very dysfunctional home.

No matter what, I couldn't please her, and when I discovered alcohol I didn't have to please anyone. Once I picked up a drink I was an alcoholic from day one. A falling down, black out, puking drunk. I only drank for eleven years, and I felt worthless.

I married a man to try to please my mother, and I loved him as a brother but not as an intimate partner, so to me sex was horrible because of that. I grew up Catholic and thought I was doomed for Hell, and spent my early years trying to hide from God because I was so ashamed of who I was.

One day I called AA and went to my first meeting scared out of my wits and feeling this was the absolute last resort. Thinking I was not so bad because I didn't sleep on a park bench, but every night I slept on the bathroom floor. I was a closet drinker, and I didn't drive. I could have been charged with impaired stroller walker.

I felt from my first meeting there was magic in the room and felt safe and didn't feel judged and criticized. It felt like people loved me just the way I was. When I walked into the meeting and felt the magic, I felt that people understood me and that they wanted me to get the program. Let's put it this way, the only safe place was at a meeting.

I couldn't wait to get to my next meeting. When I told my husband, he said, don't let them brainwash you. For the first two months I secretly went to meetings because my husband didn't want me to go. He made me swear to secrecy because he thought that if anyone knew what I was he would lose his job as a teacher. When I went home from a meeting, to my first husband, I felt judged and criticized, and that is how I felt growing up. That didn't make me feel good about myself. I felt so ashamed.

My first husband and I went to marriage counseling, and the bottom line was I married him to please my mom, and that was no reason to get married. I was desperate to make my mom happy, and there was no reason to please him. Needless to say, I felt like I had a choice to be married to AA or married to him, and I felt that AA was the only way I could stay sober. So I choose AA and separated from my husband.

I became involved with someone in the program and was with him for six and a half years. At the time I was naïve. He was a charmer and was sober for thirteen years; he made me feel like I was okay. We went to counseling, very briefly, and that didn't go well. The guy said that he was not going to waste any more of our time. Then I went for treatment for co-dependency. Going to a family treatment program was hugely helpful and assisted me to establish better boundaries. I can't do anything for others. I can only encourage things. Just because someone has long-term sobriety doesn't mean that they are good. We separated.

After him I thought, no more, no more. I was determined not to get into a relationship. But I met someone else in the program and neither of us were looking for a relationship. However, as time went on he pushed me and pushed me, and eventually we got together and that relationship was very good. He was so sweet; it was such a shock to be cared for that way. We were together happily until he died. After he died I went to grief counseling.

Then I married someone else, also in the program, and we have been together for twenty-three years. I will be sober thirty-seven years this year. And now this relationship, I would say that this one is even healthier. We downsized and have no debt, and it helped, and now we live in the country.

One of the biggest problems was that I didn't know how to do relationships.

Growing up, I didn't see a happy relationship, and transferred all my fears into my relationships. AA helps us with true intimacy, where we can share our feelings and realize that a feeling is just a feeling. For so many years in the program I would share my feelings, and if someone was angry I took it personally. Anger was the emotion I was terrified of as a child. My mother was a dry drunk. Her dad was an alcoholic, and she was in a rage all the time. I was so afraid of that rage it has taken me a long, long time to learn that it's their stuff, not mine. I also go to Al Anon.

I had an addiction to men. Sometime people just look for love in the wrong places. We see love romanticized on TV and that is not love. With men, I got help through study groups. Love is a decision.

I'm still addicted to chocolate, ice cream, and sugar in general. If I have a box of chocolates I say I'm going to have one, but I won't. I quit smoking, I went from one pack a day to three packs a day, and I couldn't breathe. Using the twelve steps I quit smoking. Chocolate and ice cream, I still occasionally will have it but I'm aware of my powerlessness, and make sure there is not too much in the house.

Working with new people is another important component. I am sponsoring eight people now. They are sober from two years to thirty-five years. I just love them and they inspire me, and that is what I need to keep out of Sue's head. I had a sponsee that I spent an awful lot of time with, almost every week, and out of the blue she fired me. She did it in a very horrible way. It kind of broke my heart. I thought of her like a daughter, that is how much I loved her, and it made me go really deep inside. Knowing that if I'm disturbed, the problem lies with me, so I looked inside. I am glad it happened because it almost forced me to change. As with all pain, it pushes us to new heights. It's our greatest motivator. I also had a sponsor and still do. When I moved I got another sponsor.

As far as today goes, it is important for me to maintain my spiritual condition. My journey in AA was a long, hard, painful process of learning what my truth was. Learning that I had to change my concept of God, because how could I have a relationship with someone I was hiding from? Prayer and meditation every day is important and I am extremely disciplined with that and do that about ½ hour. Sometimes I can just drive myself mad trying to find answers, so I'm just quiet, and they come. I had to unlearn everything I knew about God. The process of recovery is about unlearning many things. *A Course in Miracles*, I do that, and it's helpful. Another lesson that I used to help myself get into it was to read *A Return to Love*. It is easier than *A Course in Miracles* – basically there are only two emotions, fear and love, and fear is not real. This is a how I maintain my spiritual condition.

Going to meetings, I am reminded of what it was like, how hard it was, and how painful it was when I came in. I still go to two or three meetings a week. I never took a hiatus. There were not a lot of women with long-term sobriety, and I didn't like women back then. I had living problems. It felt like someone took the skin off my body. That was how painful it was, and the pain helped me want to work the steps.

I frequently go through the steps. Now it usually takes the form of working the steps with a newcomer. For the first twenty years, I had step study groups in my home. The last one was five or six years ago. Right now I am working with a new sponsee, and we are going through the steps - step by step, and she shares and I share. Each time I do them, it brings me deeper into myself and I am always learning something new. Recently I learned that there was something from my childhood that would push a button. It shocked me at the time because I thought I dealt with everything there was. I was able to take that little child and embrace her and give her the love she didn't feel she got when she was growing up. For me it is important to always be working the steps. There is always something new to learn.

The slogans, I wanted to pick up a chair and smash them to the ground, especially the *think, think, think* - I wanted to don't, don't, don't. *But for the Grace of God* made me think of the amount of people who went out and drank and died. If I got the urge I would say, I will drink tomorrow, but tomorrow never comes. Just for today helped.

And I made amends to my mom. Prayer and God's timing is everything, and I said, Mom I'm so sorry I didn't turn out to be the daughter you would have wanted me to be. She broke into tears and told me the horrible story of her childhood. I only felt love toward her, and she ended up getting terminal cancer and within two years she was dead. I am grateful that I made that amend.

One amend didn't go well that was to my first husband, and his response was not to speak to him again, so I've been to weddings and don't speak to him.

My daughter said, Mom when are you going to make amends to me? I said I'm making a living amend. My two girls were very little and don't remember me drinking. The boys have never seen me drink. I was able to take the principles of the program and put it into place with the kids. What I saw and needed to heal was to be loved and accepted for what I was. Admitting you're wrong is important. My mother never admitted she was wrong and expected us to be perfect. I had no trouble saying I made a mistake.

There are some random things that helped. Number one is honesty and getting out of the denial; It is vital to recovery. If I didn't go to meetings I might not drink, but my thinking would be off. Working with others is helpful. Responding to sponsees asking for help. Giving thanks, feeling grateful, and never forgetting where you came from: These are all key to long-term sobriety. AA was the biggest blessing in my life.

Karen – 32 Years

I'm no different from any other alcoholic. I felt different and didn't fit in, and it turned out that I was a lesbian, in a different world back then. It was less accepting. It took me until twenty-five before I accepted that being lesbian was not a passing phase. At the age of thirteen I started drinking, and drank until I was thirty-seven. My mother had sent me to the store and instead I spent the entire day drinking my friend's mother's gin. By the time I came home my mother was beside herself. It was totally out of character for me. I was very responsible. There was a confrontation, and it became violent with both of us wailing on each other, and it didn't improve after that. There were some nice times. I went on vacation and sipped cognac. When I was not getting the attention that I thought I deserved in my relationships, I would become violent. I was not always violent I could go seven years without being violent.

One morning I got up and looked in the mirror and said, you are nothing but a goddam alcoholic. When I looked in the mirror I was suicidal, drinking, and crying. On my birthday we had a storm. I had previously watched a movie called *Young at Heart* with Doris Day. In the movie there was a bad thunderstorm, and the actor shut off the window shield wipers in the car. He got in an accident and lived. I did the same in a blizzard and lived.

I used to drink just enough to live. One day I went to my ex-girlfriend, and she suggested that maybe I should stop drinking for six months, and when her daughter was sixteen we could start drinking again. The next day I came home, and I couldn't sleep, and there was a commercial that said, are you lonely? It went on and on about being lonely, and I thought it was a dating service, and I thought if I paid attention I could get a date.

It was an advertisement for AA. The morning comes, and I get dressed and write down, 10:00 AA. My brain was mush. No way I could have thought to do this, but I phoned AA at 10:00 and they said, do you think you have a drinking problem? It was the answering service and I gave them my name and work number, and my secretary called, there was a woman on the phone named Muriel. She said, hi, my name is Muriel, and I'm an alcoholic. I wanted to throw the phone. I thought, I have enough of my own problems. Then she says, did you call AA, and I said yes, and I told her about the commercial message about being lonely. She said alcoholism is a lonely disease, and that night was my first computer date with thirty-five people at AA.

They told me about the steps. I had already done the first part of the first step. The unmanageable part of the first step caused a light bulb to go off. I lost control over the booze, and my life was all fucked up; that became my mantra when I didn't feel good, and I would repeat it all over again.

The other thing that meeting gave me was hope. People also mentioned God, and I thought, oh shit. I didn't know what I got myself into, but I didn't argue. There was a group of women who said, we are going to a meeting, and told me the location and day, so I went. When it came to the second step, the power greater than me was going to be these women. So that was the second step.

Then I went to meetings in Toronto, and someone said if you don't do step two then you are in trouble, and I said, oh shit. I started reading the AA book *Came to Believe*, and I thought, oh why did she give me this book because it was a bunch of people having the DTs. Part of the way through the book a woman said the God of her understanding was her father, and I thought, what is it that your birth father wants for you? Health and happiness and that is all that any parent wants for you. So I could accept that, and it wasn't that

I didn't have a God of my understanding, but I wasn't going to turn my will over until I knew what his will was for me. The book really helped me. There were a bunch of other things that I had to do, like go to meetings, get a sponsor, sponsor others and do the steps.

When it came to the 4**th,** my pen took off, and I started writing and writing. There were four of us in the family, and I was born after the war, and my brother was born before. My dad had been off to war for five years, and my mother was basically a single mom. When he came back, she got pregnant with me. It was an adjustment for her. I was a sick kid, and they used to wrap kids in angora wool, and I cried a lot because I was allergic to the material. This was what came out of the fourth step. Basically, I was punishing her for World War Two. My brother and my mother developed a bond and closeness that I didn't have. When my dad came back, he was not the same man, and now they had a baby that was sickly. It took my mom time to adjust, and by the time she did I was five, and I didn't feel she loved me. I know that today she loved me very much, but it took a long time before I could accept that. There were times in my twenties when we fought a lot, and then there were times I thought she was superwoman. Finally, in sobriety, I could allow her to be a human being, and it made for a much nicer relationship. During the fourth and fifth I forgave her. I had self-centered down forty-nine times. A good part of my life I wondered why I was a lesbian.

For the fifth step I didn't trust many people, so I went to a psychologist because she was sworn to secrecy by law. I did the fifth step with her. The thing is at this time I've shared anything I told her, so what I felt at the time was a big secret really wasn't that big a deal.

Step seven is to humbly ask him to remove our shortcomings. Everything I wrote down was my shortcoming and they were all in the past. For the next couple years it was pretty bad, and I could see how these character defects would come and control my behaviour. It took me a long time of trying to control my emotions. First I had to allow myself to feel them. The first time I went dancing sober I had to talk to myself and say how many people paid to watch you dance? And the answer was none. Then I asked myself what is the worst thing that can happen? And the answer was, if someone danced with the person I brought and she went home with that person. So I talked myself out of the anxiety. Then I continued working on the next steps.

There are some years I can go along nicely and then boom, it comes out again, and I act just like I was fifteen again.

When it came to making amends, I used a list of people that had hurt me, and what I did as a result. That method caused me to leave out abandonment. My ex-girlfriend that lived with me for ten years, we had her daughter part-time and to this day I am called Mom by her. It was a couple years that I had not seen her, and when I opened the door she was there and we hugged and cried and hugged and cried, and I realized at that moment that I was needing to make an amend.

Another amend was to a girl that lied about her age when she was fifteen to get into a gay club. We dumped her. Again, that was abandonment. She was just trying to find a place she fit in. The ones that were on the paper were simple, and what I was apologizing for were my actions.

My friend who shared a house with me but moved back home, that amends was not that I got drunk and did something. It was more that we were best friends and she was moving back home with her parents. I was pissed and I treated her terribly instead of realizing what she was going through. I was not much of a best friend either. She wanted to move home and try to not be gay but I was not sensitive to that. It was a nice feeling to make amends.

I keep in contact with a God of my understanding and I pray before I even get out of bed. I get a coffee and go back to bed and have a chat with God. I'm not good at meditating because I have a hard time staying still. I often fall asleep during commercials. That is just the way I am. Improving our conscious contact with

God that evolves through hard times and good times.

Those ladies that took me under my wing, they were helpful. One was the Betty, the Chair at the Guelph convention, and I saw a bunch of people walking around with purple ribbons, and asked, how do you get those purple ribbons, and I did whatever she did. I was treasurer for AA, I sponsored people, just this weekend I gave a woman her medallion and I felt special about being part of her sobriety. And there is another woman who calls me to talk and she never says good-bye without saying I love you. The pink cloud comes back when working with others. One woman said, when I cried you helped. It gave me a good feeling.

The fellowship of AA helped me achieve this length of sobriety. Even in my first years I was surrounded with the AA fellowship. I met my wife there. I have friends outside the program. They are not the type I would have chummed around when I was drinking. That feeling of belonging got me to stay. That is my life. There is no way to separate it.

The people that go and don't stay clean and sober separate the two. This is my life. A lot of what I do is with people in AA. My best friend is in AA. I go to garage sales and take trips to Florida with people in AA. The people I sponsor, we go to the breakfast club, and nutrition for learning. Those friendships that I developed in

AA became part and parcel of my life, the same with when I was drinking I only hung around with people who drank. In AA I mimicked people until it hit home. I also worked the steps.

In my first year I hug around with a woman, and she had just celebrated a year, and she told me about being in and out of the program, and I asked, what made you stay? She said when she was in and out she had thrown out the God part. So I knew that would be a part of my life. I started hanging out with women and got a sponsor.

I went to counseling my first year. I went to an employee assistance program a month after I joined AA, and I saw that woman in my first year of sobriety. I did the fifth step and brought her to a closed discussion. She was a really nice lady.

I had other addictions. I smoked until January of 2000, and I had buried both parents with lung cancer, and an aunt had died that way. I tried to quit many times. I joined a gym and quit at the same time. I used the twelve steps to help me quit. I did a fourth step around the smoking. I couldn't stand shoveling the food in my mouth when I would quit. After a year I celebrated with not going to the gym. It was a slip and slide process for the weight gain. I never went back to smoking. If I turned on the TV now and they said the world was going to an end tomorrow I wouldn't drink but I would smoke. I also love sugar and liked chocolate.

I also made changes in my recreation. I had people that would come over and we would play Trivial Pursuit. After I quit smoking I went to house tours. Some of my neighbours were in a play, so I went to entertainment plays. I found out that if I want to eat what I wanted to eat when I want to eat it that I should join senior aerobics. I walk the hills with people that I used to work with. We bike and walk the trails.

Early in my sobriety, the first 10 years, if something really bad happened and I got angry I would say, "fucked if they were going to get my sobriety." Now I'm thinking that when I'm going to meet my master, I'm going to do it sober.

I've had problems with my wife and I've had problems at work and I've gone to couples counseling and Employee Assistance Program. When push comes to shove I look for something to solve it. I can't think of anything specific. We have been together twenty-seven or twenty-eight years, so we've had problems.

I walked away from meetings for a while too. After we bought the house we had problems in a group and we wandered away. I still had AA people coming in and out of my life. One Sunday I went to an AA meeting and a man I knew was there. My sponsor had died. When I retired I went to the Sunday group and I came out after the meeting and said, whatever possessed me to go there? For some strange reason I went there again. There was a woman there at her first meeting, and suddenly I felt at home and became active all over again.

Six or seven years ago I found out that during the times I wasn't going to meetings I did a lot of damage and I wasn't aware of it. I wasn't aware of the problems I was creating in our life.

I drank because I couldn't stand the emotions as a teenager. I like the feel-good emotions. I've learned some things, like just because I'm feeling guilty doesn't mean I am guilty. Mothers have a way of making you feel guilty. With grief you have to let it run its course. It takes as long as it takes. With anxiety, it affects my entire bowels and stomach. With it, prayer is the only thing I found that seems to help that one. I can't do anything about the fact that I have emotions. Drinking never got rid of my emotions. That is why I went to AA. First, emotions just came in slowly and then I spent five years to try to control them. Then fight or flight mechanism comes off with everything. If I was feeling jealous I would follow it through and say, do you feel like dying? No, so I would ask myself, what is the problem? I felt nervous when I began having sex sober.

No matter what happens in life I was doing things for me. What is in it for Karen? If I go out and bring my wife home a chocolate bar, I do it because I want her to love me. I wanted to show her that I love her. I accept that my motive is selfish and accept it and concentrate on the behaviour. Mother Teresa did the same thing. She wanted to get a better spot in heaven.

It's attraction you mimic until you get it. You have to know people who are married a long-time to mimic that. You take a little bit of this person and a little bit about that person and think, this is who I'm going to become. It is based on attraction. Christian people show me they are Christian.

Betty – 35 years

The women that I met when I first came into AA helped me to accept myself as an alcoholic. Once I met those gals everything was smooth sailing. I never had a missed step. I joined a meeting on a Tuesday night. I have had one sponsor, she is ninety-three, ten years older than me, and has seven years more sobriety than me. She is in a nursing home but still gets out to some meetings, although we are not getting around that well now with our health issues.

When you go back to the beginning, my husband passed away when he was forty-seven. I had five kids. The oldest was twenty-one, and the youngest was eleven. My husband was a drinker. I had lots of resentment when he passed away. Prior to his illness, I was never much of a drinker. He had cancer of the pancreas. I couldn't go to the hospital without a shot. A self-employed businessman, he kept working as long as he was able. He wouldn't let me talk about his cancer and shut me right out. The only thing that that helped was for me to drown my sorrows.

I was teaching, so I handed in my resignation. This enabled me to be off work when he was into the bad part of the sickness. He had started to add a room on at the back of the house, and we had our first Christmas in that room. We were sitting in the back room and I said, honey you looked yellow. The solvents that he put on the floor made him sicker. His illness progressed and he got sicker and passed away March 27, 1980. I really went down hill. I was not taking care of the house and my boys were worried about me. Throughout this time I kept praying, and praying, and praying.

On my birthday friends said, we are taking you to the detoxification centre. It was horrible. It was in the old building. I hated to go to the washroom, I was so afraid that I would push those doors and get out and get a drink. The third day I took a shower, and I picked up a book called *Our Daily Bread,* and I opened up to a page that said that God does not always work directly with us. He works through others. I felt something warm go through my whole body. So I never mentioned it at meetings, but I do discuss it with some people that believe in spiritual experiences like that. Since then I have never had the desire to drink.

One of the women who worked in the detoxification centre wanted me to stay. But I had to go for an emergency dental appointment. I went and made a decision I was going to go home and do what I was supposed to do. I started stripping the beds. It was a beautiful day, and I went every morning to AA and in the evenings too. As time went on I became a General Service Representative (GSR) and went to area meetings and did that well into my sobriety. At one convention I convened and was the chairperson. You meet different people there. I met some great people and we became close.

Throughout the years some of my friends were passing away, and after my mother died in 1989, I decided to go back to teaching. My husband had not been able to provide that much as he did not expect to die so young. My oldest son got married the following September. I was still going to meetings, working, taking care of the kids, and it got to be so much that I started to slack off on the meetings. At the time I had twenty years of sobriety. My sponsor and I still went out to meetings we just slowed down. As I got away from meetings, going back was uncomfortable but I kept working, and I didn't drink. That is the main thing, no matter what. Finally, all my boys were married.

I developed fibromyalgia, and getting around was difficult, but AA and the principles are in your mind all the time. If someone called me up and needed me to talk to them, I would be there. I just do what I know I have to do now. I have twelve grandchildren and two great-grandchildren. Today I called my one granddaughter and said, I remember when you were born, and reminisced with her. That is the benefit of being sober. I am participating in those events. I was involved with my family. We had a cottage, and we went up there. While staying at the cottage, I would go to meetings all the times with my youngest son. The people at the AA meetings, they would look forward to the next time summer when I would visit again. You don't think you have said anything special, but it means something to someone.

Being active, staying active, and respecting old timers, sitting and having coffee with them, it helps. Sometimes my sponsor still gets a call. I did all the steps. When I did my inventory I sat in my back room and we talked, and talked, and talked. I made amends all the time, and I'm so grateful, and my children are thankful that I found AA. I never prayed so hard in my whole life to try and get sober; it's the hardest thing to do. I just needed it to cope with what was going on with my life at the time.

I was on the board for a recovery home. My involvement included setting things up and doing shopping. I had the time, and I was so active picking up girls at the bus or train station; they were scared. It was a great time in my sobriety.

Throughout my life my hobbies were gardening and cooking and I still do these today. I have my children and grandchildren over to the house for every holiday; all together we are over thirty. My kids are in and out of here all the time, and I'm so close to my grandchildren, and I often think if I hadn't stopped I couldn't have been doing any of that. Even teaching, I always taught kindergarten. I have been singing in the choir for fifty-five years. It is something I've enjoyed doing very much, it has always been a part of my life. I would be so upset with myself if I couldn't do that because active alcoholism doesn't allow you to do those things.

There was one Christmas dinner when my husband was ill, and I couldn't get a dinner on the table then. Not like I do now, if I had missed all those years with my children and grandchildren that would have been awful. Just this morning I sang happy birthday to my granddaughter early in the morning. I am grateful to be able to do that.

My son, the youngest, is a counselor and he has groups with AA men and learned a lot about alcoholism. When his father died, he was eleven and was looking after me. It was less than a year ago that he said, mom, did I ever thank you for getting sober; you have no idea how much it meant to me. When we went to the cottage, there were so many things that I was able to do with him, if I had not have been sober, he would have missed so much. To come and thank me, it was a tearjerker. They don't worry about me. Sobriety has an impact. I owe it to God and AA. I'm a staunch AA member.

There is this one guy that comes on the radio, and he says, I used to be an addict, and I'm not anymore; that is what we call stinky thinking. He may be recovered, but he is always an alcoholic.

Easy does it was a good slogan for me. I never had the urge to drink after that spiritual experience. I never had the urge to drink. I had my water or coffee. It was unbelievable to think how bad it was for me. Easy does it was the slogan I used.

I am thirty-five years sober this month. There was never a need for me to use that *One Day at a Time* AA slogan; I got so involved with the things I was doing, and life is too good to go back to that crap. I never had to pray for the desire to be removed because from that day I felt the warmth go through my body while in the detoxification centre I never wanted to drink again. Your life is entirely different, and it's a great thing to be able to depend on myself. I know that I can trust myself and be around alcohol without having a desire. My boys drink, but they don't have a problem.

I come from a heritage of drinking. My father and my grandfather were alcoholics, my uncles were alcoholics, and my mother had a problem. One day I was out teaching, and one of my boys was sick, so they were home for the day and had heard something creeping up the steps, and there was my mother pulling a chair over and getting the liquor out of the cupboard, and we would find bottles; I never saw her tipsy but she must have been. My dad, he used to own an apartment downtown, and he used to keep a bottle on the bricks. I never saw him tipsy.

I remember speaking at meetings. I was so scared but I had an uncle who really supported me at AA meeting until he passed away.

I made lots of friends, women particularly; I always thought if they are alcoholic it's okay for me to be; because they were people I respected and looked up to. We had so much fun together and became a real club. Some men we socialized with too, but mostly with women, they were so nice and I admired them so much. We had a lot of nice women in our AA group meeting.

My sponsor is still my sponsor all these years; she is the only one I had. I have had a few sponsees; one lives in another city and still calls me. Life has been good because of AA.

THE 12-STEPS OF ALCOHOLICS ANONYMOUS

1. We admitted we were powerless over alcohol – that our lives had become unmanageable.

2. Came to believe that a Power greater than ourselves could restore us to sanity.

3. Made a decision to turn our will and our lives over to the care of God as we understood Him.

4. Made a searching and fearless moral inventory of ourselves.

5. Admitted to God, to ourselves and to another human being the exact nature of our wrongs.

6. Were entirely ready to have God remove all these defects of character.

7. Humbly asked Him to remove our shortcomings.

8. Made a list of all persons we had harmed, and became willing to make amends to them all.

9. Made direct amends to such people wherever possible, except when to do so would injure them or others.

10. Continued to take personal inventory and when we were wrong promptly admitted it.

11. Sought through prayer and meditation to improve our conscious contact with

God as we understood Him, praying only for knowledge of His will for us and the power to carry that out.

12. Having had a spiritual awakening as the result of these steps, we tried to carry this message to alcoholics and to practice these principles in all our affairs. (Alcoholics Anonymous, 1939)

REFERENCES

Alcoholics Anonymous: The big book --4th ed.--. (2001). New York City, NY: Alcoholics Anonymous World Services.

Alcoholics Anonymous. (2016.). *Estimated worldwide A.A. individual and Group membership.* doi:http://www.aa.org/assets/en_US/smf-132_en.pdf (NTIS)

Brown, R. A., Abrantes, A. M., Read, J. P., Marcus, B. H., Jakicic, J., Strong, D. R., . . . Gordon, A. A. (2008). Aerobic Exercise for Alcohol Recovery: Rationale, Program Description, and Preliminary Findings. *Behavior Modification, 33*(2), 220-249. doi:10.1177/0145445508329112

Caetano, R. (1987). Public opinions about alcoholism and its treatment. *J. Stud. Alcohol Journal of Studies on Alcohol, 48*(2), 153-160. doi:10.15288/jsa.1987.48.153

Costello, R.M. (1975). Alcoholism treatment and evaluation, II: Collation of Two Year Follow-up studies. *International Journal of Addictions.* 10, 857–867.

Diclemente, C. C., & Scott, C. W. (1997). Stages of Change: Interactions With Treatment Compliance and Involvement. *PsycEXTRA Dataset.* doi:10.1037/e495632006-008

Fiorentine, R. & Hillhouse, M.P. (2000). Drug treatment and 12-step program participation: The additive effects of integrated recovery activities. *Journal of Substance Abuse Treatment*, 18, 65-74.

Fortuna, J. L. (2010). Sweet Preference, Sugar Addiction and the Familial History of Alcohol Dependence: Shared Neural Pathways and Genes. *Journal of Psychoactive Drugs, 42*(2), 147-151.

Hall, S. M., Havassy, B. E., & Wasserman, D. A. (1991). Effects of commitment to abstinence, positive moods, stress, and coping on relapse to cocaine use. *Journal of Consulting and Clinical Psychology, 59*(4), 526-532.

Hammer, S. B., Ruby, C. L., Brager, A. J., Prosser, R. A., & Glass, J. D. (2010). Environmental Modulation of Alcohol Intake in Hamsters: Effects of Wheel Running and Constant Light Exposure. *Alcoholism: Clinical and Experimental Research, 34*(9), 1651-1658.

Fortuna, J. L. (2010). Sweet Preference, Sugar Addiction and the Familial History of Alcohol Dependence: Shared Neural Pathways and Genes. *Journal of Psychoactive Drugs, 42*(2), 147-151.

Havassy, B. E., Wasserman, D. A., & Hall, S. M. (1993). Relapse to Cocaine Use: Conceptual Issues. *PsycEXTRA Dataset.*

Humphreys K, Mavis BE, Stöffelmayr BE. Are twelve-step programs appropriate for disenfranchised groups? Evidence from a study of posttreatment mutual help group Involvement. *Prevention in Human Services.* 1994;11:165–180.

Humphreys, K., Mankowski, E. S., Moos, R. H., & Finney, J. W. (1999). Do enhanced friendship networks and active coping mediate the effect of self-help groups on substance abuse? *Annals of Behavioral Medicine Ann. Behav. Med., 21*(1), 54-60. doi:10.1007/bf02895034

Humphreys, K., Moos, R. H., & Cohen, C. (1997). Social and community resources and long-term recovery from treated and untreated alcoholism. *J. Stud. Alcohol Journal of Studies on Alcohol, 58*(3), 231-238. doi:10.15288/jsa.1997.58.231

Laudet A, Magura S, Vogel H, Knight E. Support, mutual aid and recovery from dual diagnosis. *Community Mental Health Journal.* 2000;36(5):457–476.

Laudet, A. B., Savage, R., & Mahmood, D. (2002). Pathways to Long-Term Recovery: A Preliminary Investigation. *Journal of Psychoactive Drugs, 34*(3), 305-311. doi:10.1080/02791072.2002.10399968

Moos, R. H., & Moos, B. S. (2006). Participation in treatment and Alcoholics Anonymous: A 16-year follow-up of initially untreated individuals. *Journal of Clinical Psychology J. Clin. Psychol., 62*(6), 735-750. doi:10.1002/jclp.20259

Moos, R. H., & Moos, B. S. (2007). Protective resources and long-term recovery from alcohol use disorders. *Drug and Alcohol Dependence, 86*(1), 46-54. doi:10.1016/j.drugalcdep.2006.04.015

Murphy, T. J., Pagano, R. R., & Marlatt, G. (1986). Lifestyle modification with heavy alcohol drinkers: Effects of aerobic exercise and meditation. *Addictive Behaviors, 11*(2), 175-186. doi:10.1016/0306-4603(86)90043-2

Polcin, D. L., Korcha, R., Bond, J., & Galloway, G. (2010). What Did We Learn from Our Study on Sober Living Houses and Where Do We Go from Here? *Journal of Psychoactive Drugs, 42*(4), 425-433. doi:10.1080/02791072.2010.10400705

Sandoz, J. (2014). Finding God through the Spirituality of the 12 Steps of Alcoholics Anonymous. *Religions, 5*(4), 948-960. doi:10.3390/rel5040948

Sinyor, D., Brown, T., Rostant, L., & Seraganian, P. (1982). The role of a physical fitness program in the treatment of alcoholism. *J. Stud. Alcohol Journal of Studies on Alcohol, 43*(3), 380-386. doi:10.15288/jsa.1982.43.380

Snow, M. G., Prochaska, J. O., & Rossi, J. S. (1994). Processes of change in Alcoholics Anonymous: Maintenance factors in long-term sobriety. *J. Stud. Alcohol Journal of Studies on Alcohol, 55*(3), 362-371. doi:10.15288/jsa.1994.55.362

Timko, C., Finney, J. W., Moos, R. H., & Moos, B. S. (1995). Short-term treatment careers and outcomes of previously untreated alcoholics. *J. Stud. Alcohol Journal of Studies on Alcohol, 56*(6), 597-610. doi:10.15288/jsa.1995.56.597

Timko, C., Moos, R. H., Finney, J. W., & Lesar, M. D. (2000). Long-term outcomes of alcohol use disorders: Comparing untreated individuals with those in alcoholics anonymous and formal treatment. *J. Stud. Alcohol Journal of Studies on Alcohol, 61*(4), 529-540. doi:10.15288/jsa.2000.61.529

Trivedi, M. H., Greer, T. L., Grannemann, B. D., Church, T. S., Somoza, E., Blair, S. N., ... Nunes, E. (2011). Stimulant Reduction Intervention using Dosed Exercise (STRIDE) - CTN 0037: Study protocol for a randomized controlled trial. *Trials, 12*(1), 206. doi:10.1186/1745-6215-12-206

Vaillant, G. E. (1995). *The natural history of alcoholism revisited*. Cambridge, MA: Harvard University Press.

REHAB HELPDESK

Vision

Our vision is for people not to fear Addiction.

Mission

Our mission is to provide free objective: education, guidance, and support to anyone affected by Addiction. This includes not only sufferers, but also anyone they directly affect: family, friends, health workers, co-workers, etc.

We aim to educate with workshops, learning programs, group sessions, and free online resources. We will offer

Guidance and Support. Our helpdesk service will offer free, objective guidance from qualified staff. Callers will often be referred to specialist service providers that meet their specific needs. We also provide similar programs for other issues that affect the mind, such as Depression, Anxiety, PTSD, Eating Disorders, and Post-Natal Depression.

No matter how much it hurts now, one day you will look back and realize it changed your life for the better.

—Anonymous

www.ingramcontent.com/pod-product-compliance
Lightning Source LLC
Chambersburg PA
CBHW060521080526
44586CB00012B/558